PLANT CLOSURES

MYTHS, REALITIES AND RESPONSES

BY

GILDA HAAS

&

PLANT CLOSURES PROJECT

EDITOR: HOLLY SKLAR

DESIGNER: MICHAEL PROKOSCH
ORIGINAL DESIGN CREATOR: CYNTHIA CARR
TABLES & BOXES: GILDA HAAS & HOLLY SKLAR

SOUTH END PRESS
PAMPHLET NO. 3

LIST OF TABLES AND BOXES

Cover Photo By Paul Chell, **Youngstown Vindicator**
Copyright © 1985 by Gilda Haas and Plant Closures Project
Library of Congress Cataloging in Publication Data
Hass, Gilda.
    Plant closures.
    (Pamphlet/South End Press: no. 3)
    Bibliography: p.
    1. Plant shutdowns—United States—Case studies.
I. Plant Closures Project (Calif.) II. Title.
III. Series: Pamphlet (South End Press); no. 3.
HD5708.55.U6H33 1985   338.6'042   85-27925
ISBN 0-89608-212-1

Special thanks to Jan Gilbrecht of the Plant Closures Project for her assistance in
researching, writing and producing this booklet; to Ellen Green for her role in
conceptualizing the intitial project and commenting on subsequent drafts of the
manuscript; to Susan Schacher of the Plant Closures Project for her invaluable help
in the development of the booklet; and to all those who were interviewed, enriching
this publication. Thanks also to Kathy Seal and Joan Trafecanty for their interviews
with the Ontario workers; Ruthann Evanoff; and South End Press.

TABLE OF CONTENTS

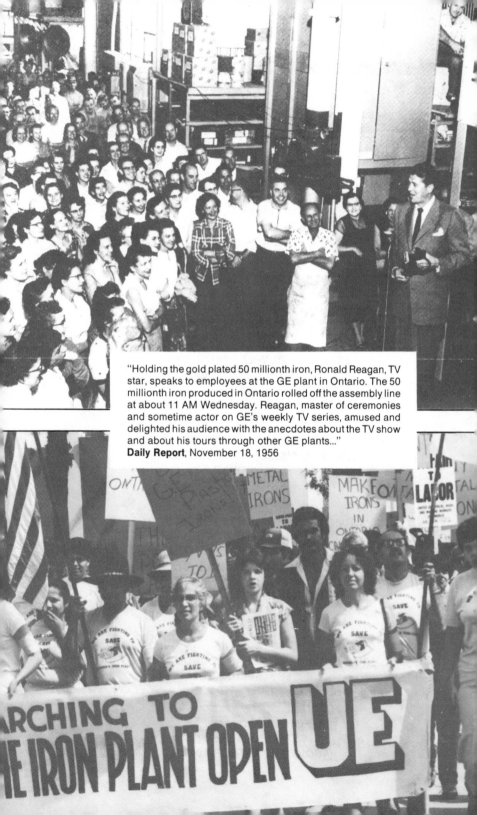

"Holding the gold plated 50 millionth iron, Ronald Reagan, TV star, speaks to employees at the GE plant in Ontario. The 50 millionth iron produced in Ontario rolled off the assembly line at about 11 AM Wednesday. Reagan, master of ceremonies and sometime actor on GE's weekly TV series, amused and delighted his audience with the anecdotes about the TV show and about his tours through other GE plants..."
Daily Report, November 18, 1956

BRINGING GOOD THINGS TO GE

These words appeared on the headstone when workers held a mock funeral outside General Electric's flat-iron plant in Ontario, California. They were burying a metal iron to protest the plant shutdown in February 1982. Little more than two years earlier, the plant was celebrating a production record of five million irons, supplying 60 percent of the world's flat-iron market and making more profit than any of GE's other small appliance divisions.[1] Yet, even then there were warning signs of a plant shutdown. Machinery went unrepaired and spare parts inventories were reduced. The paint department was closed, models were eliminated from the assembly line and overtime was cut back.

In 1980, Mary McDaniel, president of the plant's United Electrical Workers (UE) Local 1012, noticed that GE had dropped its ads for the metal iron produced in Ontario from the trade journals. Later that year, she learned that GE planned to open two new metal iron factories in Mexico and Brazil, and was already producing a plastic travel iron in a non-union plant in North Carolina. A new line of plastic-bodied irons, designed by Ontario engineers, would be produced in Singapore.

Worried about the plant's future, McDaniel organized a meeting with representatives of the Los Angeles Coalition Against Plant Shutdowns (LACAPS), a coalition of religious, labor and community people who came together in response to closures in the Los Angeles auto, steel and rubber industries. LACAPS advised the Ontario workers to join forces with others in the area who would also suffer from a major loss of jobs and investment. As a result of this November 1980 meeting, a broad community-labor committee was organized to investigate the possibility of a GE closure and develop a plan of action. GE, meanwhile, had just assured the Mayor of Ontario that the company had no intention of closing the plant.[2]

Premeditated Murder

On July 20, 1981, the news hit Ontario. A GE closure notice accompanied that week's paychecks. Layoffs would begin as early as September and the plant would shut down in February 1982. Ontario's 80-year history as the "flat-iron capital of the world" would be coming to an abrupt end.

"It was just like someone in the family had passed away," said Bob Bale, who worked in the plant along with his father, brother and two children. Bale observed, "They could come out here on a jet airliner one day and say, 'We're going to shut down,' and leave all these people hanging. I think its pretty sadistic."[3]

Shocked by the GE announcement, the Ontario City Council passed a resolution urging the company to reconsider. The community-labor committee had forged a broad alliance, and together with City Council members, the Mayor, local trade unions, church pastors, electric and gas company officials and the United Way, they placed an ad in the local paper, accusing GE of running away for greater profits and urging GE president John Welch to keep the plant open. While unionized GE workers in Ontario were paid an average of $8 per hour in 1982, non-union GE workers in North Carolina earned half as much, at about $4 per hour. Workers in Brazil and Singapore were paid even less: $1.73 and $1.09 an hour.

In July 1981, 2,000 people marched through downtown Ontario, demanding that GE keep the plant open or sell it to another company that would. Boris Block, secretary-treasurer of the UE, told the crowd: "Old-timers will remember the GE slogan, 'Progress is our most important product.' Hogwash! Profits are their most important product."[4]

Ontario citizens had plenty of reasons to join GE workers in their fight to save the plant. GE was the third largest employer in a city of 94,000 people, and a major employer of the area's minorities and women. In 1982, according to Mary McDaniel, 50 percent of the plant's 1,000 workers were women and 50 percent were Black or Latino/a.[5] Shock waves from the shutdown could put as many as 2,000 *more* people out of work employed by parts suppliers, supermarkets, restaurants and other businesses dependent upon plant orders and customer paychecks. In a series of "ripple effects," retail sales would drop and other businesses would be forced to close; the local tax base would

hereth

LNS

shrink, causing cutbacks and layoffs in the public sector; social services and charitable contributions would decline at a time of increasing demand. GE's annual payroll of $13 million was spent primarily in Ontario and 65 firms did regular business with the plant. Economists estimated that the total financial impact of the shutdown would come to $91 million.[6]

GE had explained the closure as a response to changing consumer demand: "GE is phasing out production of metal irons in favor of lighter plastic-bodied models which American consumers seem to prefer," said the company's community relations manager.[7] But small-appliance retailers across the country saw a high demand for the metal irons produced in Ontario, and they began stockpiling irons in order to avoid anticipated shortages.[8]

In a last-ditch effort to save the plant, the workers offered to buy it themselves. To help analyze the feasibility of a buyout, the union raised $20,000 to perform a marketing study to determine whether or not American consumers really preferred plastic irons over metal ones as GE insisted. The workers submitted a formal proposal to GE in late January 1982, but GE never seriously considered it. On February 11, GE announced that it had sold the plant for about eight million dollars to a company producing electric fans. The new owners claimed that after closing for at least nine months for retooling, they would employ up to 300 workers.[9] But at this writing, the plant is again up for sale, without ever having been reopened for production.

On February 25, 1982, the last metal iron produced in the United States moved off the assembly line and 1,000 unemployed GE workers joined 1.2 million others across the country who had lost their jobs that year from a plant closure.[10] The union's consumer study was released the day of the closure, indicating a strong consumer preference for metal irons: 72 percent of those polled in a national sample indicated that they had bought metal irons within the past year.

No Longer Needed

"They didn't even give us the dignity of shutting down like they were supposed to," recalls Judi Harris, who had worked in the plant for 16 years. "We were supposed to work until Friday, but on Thursday one of the girls called me, 'Judy, they've closed the doors on us. The foreman is standing there with a letter from the company saying that we've produced the amount of irons that they need and they've got our checks there.' They came down through the plant and told everybody to shut their machines off, turn off the lights, and get out of the plant. We had filled the quota of irons they needed for their orders and therefore we were no longer needed."

"I think the majority of us are damned mad," says Harris. "We're damn mad that GE would do this to us. After all the years that we had produced irons for General Electric and made them number one in the iron market. It was because of the pride we had in our work that they were number one."

Harris described her search for work eight months after the plant shutdown: "Well, I usually go out just about every day. I don't miss very many days, and I usually hit six or eight places a day. If they'll pay me $7 an hour to work for them, great! I'm applying for $4 an hour jobs, too. I just want a job. I think, number one, people aren't hiring. They're closing down. Number two, I think 40 isn't the most popular age to get a job."[11]

About 25 percent of the total GE workforce was over 50 years old. Their prospects for *any* future employment, much less at comparable wages and benefits, are bleak. Leona Setty had worked at GE for 10 years and was 60 years old when it shut down. She had expected to work until age 62, when she would be eligible for Social Security. Her pension from GE comes to $200 per month. "I have a house payment of $500 a month," says Setty. "It's either lose it or get a job soon. But you know I'm not going to get any great jobs at this age."[12]

E.N. Cheatham had worked at GE for over 35 years. "The shutdown cut us short of retirement by a couple of years," he explains. "You can get an early pension, but they cut off so much it isn't worth taking it. So now I was out two years without any income." Nine months after the shutdown he said, "I got 26 weeks of unemployment, but that's run out already. So I've been existing on what savings I had."[13]

Judi Harris describes the sense of isolation and growing depression experienced by an older coworker: "I have a friend in Pomona who has no family out here and she calls me three or four times a week. She's almost in tears. It's heartbreaking. She was 60 when the plant closed. She'll tell me how depressed she is. She can't stand watching that damn television anymore. I know that's why she calls me—just to have somebody to talk to. I think that's basically the way the majority of us feel. We're depressed. It's very lonely. We had a big family and now we're cut down to where we're by ourselves."

From their contacts with other workers around the state, the Ontario workers knew the dangers of severe depression following job loss. Nine workers committed suicide after the closure of the General Motors plant in Fremont, California. The closure of the GM plant in South Gate, in Los Angeles County, led to six suicides. A study published in 1977 found a suicide rate 30 times the expected number among displaced workers.[14]

Across the U.S., the human costs of plant closures are staggering. According to a 1976 study by Dr. Harvey Brenner of Johns Hopkins University (analyzing data for the 1940-1973 period), a 1 percent increase in the unemployment rate, sustained over a period of six years, is associated approximately with: 37,000 total deaths (including 20,000 cardiovascular deaths); 920 suicides; 650 homicides; 500 deaths from cirrhosis of the liver; 4,000 state mental hospital admissions; and 3,300 state prison admissions.[15] During the 1973-74 recession the unemployment rate rose 14.3 percent. In a 1984 study prepared for the Congressional Joint Economic Committee, Brenner attributes a 2.3 percent rise in the mortality rate to this recession. During the 1981-82 recession unemployment jumped from 7.2 percent in July 1981 to 10.7 percent in

Plant Closures Project

November 1982, a rise of over 48 percent. According to Brenner, the increase in deaths from this recession—appearing three to five years after the height of unemployment—could be at least three times as much as the 1973-74 recession.[16] That is, the mortality rate could rise some 7 percent or more.

Almost a year after the closure, most GE workers were still unemployed. Mary McDaniel could not find a manufacturing job, but wanting to stay in the area, she opened a restaurant. Business has not been good. Judi Harris, who has a disabled husband and children to support, went to college to learn computer programming. "I'm trying to get into a field that maybe won't put me out of a job again," she says. "But it's scary, all the plants that are shutting down and running away."[17]

Nationally, unemployment remains high among workers who lost their jobs due to plant closures or staff cuts between 1979 and 1984, according to a 1984 report by the Bureau of Labor Statistics. Among workers with at least three years on the job before dismissal, only 60 percent had found jobs by January 1984 and, of these, 45 percent were earning less money in their new jobs. Many were forced to accept steep pay cuts of 20 percent or more. The prospect for finding new employment was directly related to the age of the displaced worker. Workers 20 to 24 years old fared best, with 70 percent finding new jobs. Among workers 55 to 64 years old, only 41 percent found new jobs.[18]

Nine months after the GE closure, the impact on the Ontario community was plainly visible. Leona Setty sadly described what she saw: "You go into any of these restaurants, they're pretty much empty. When I came here in '68 there were a lot of nice stores on Euclid Avenue.

There's hardly anything there now. That's too bad because this is a nice little town, but it's going to end up a ghost town."

As the city of Ontario declined, GE posted record third-quarter earnings in 1982, showing an increase of 11 percent even though sales fell off 4 percent. GE President John Welch attributed the earnings gain to the company's "cost-cutting moves."[19] For 1983, GE was ranked fifth in net profits in the *Forbes* 500. In 1984, GE sold its overseas irons plants and other small-appliance operations to Black and Decker, a large power tool company.[20] The Black and Decker deal is part of an overall GE strategy to emphasize higher profit, high-tech products, such as military radar and communications. GE is ranked fourth on the Defense Department's list of top contractors. Drawing on $5 billion it had accumulated by selling or closing consumer-appliance plants, GE acquired new high-tech businesses in 1984 such as military electronics firms and computer companies which specialize in factory automation. As GE sees it, "the automated factory will not only be the factory of the future, but the factory most likely to have a future."[21]

Breaking New Ground

The negative impact of the Ontario closure reached beyond the workers in the plant, but the *positive* effects of the fightback campaign reached even further. The community-labor committee was able to tarnish GE's public image—nurtured by an $80 million advertising and promotion budget at the time of the closing—as a caring institution which "Brings Good Things To Life."[22] The Ontario campaign generated local, regional and national press, including a segment on the CBS program, *Sixty Minutes*, which galvanized support for the growing plant closures movement. UE Local 1012 President Mary McDaniel comments, "After the show was on *Sixty Minutes* I got letters from local, state and national elected officials congratulating us on our fight, saying that they would support plant closure legislation." "Even three years after the closure, I still get calls from people asking questions about what we did," she says. "I still meet a lot of people today, who because of their

Clay Bennett

knowledge about our fight, won't buy GE products, even though we never organized a boycott."

Although the GE workers ultimately lost their jobs, their well-publicized struggle put enormous pressure on GE and helped the United Electrical Workers win groundbreaking plant closures language in their new national contract (Westinghouse then agreed to the same provisions for its 40,000 hourly workers).[23] Under the three-year contract, which covers 78,000 employees, GE must provide the following:

*At least six months advance notice of a plant closure or of the company's intention to introduce automated machinery or robots into the factory.

*Increased severance pay for victims of plant closures. GE workers used to receive one week pay per year of service in severance pay. Under the new contract, workers with less than 15 years receive 1.5 weeks pay and workers with 15 years or more receive 2 weeks per year worked.

*Improved pension benefits for older workers.[24]

In many ways, the GE closure in Ontario is typical of the thousands of shutdowns that have rocked the lives of workers and communities across the country. What is less typical is that the workers and their community allies fought back. Judi Harris comments, "Nobody around here had put up a fight against a shutdown before. They had all just accepted the fact and let the doors close and went to the unemployment office and drew their unemployment. We did give GE one hell of a battle. We fought them tooth and nail."

Coalition building for the Ontario campaign grew far beyond the original community-labor committee. In November 1981, GE workers participated in the First Western International Conference on Economic Dislocation organized by LACAPS and other plant closure activists throughout California. Held in a Baptist church in the Los Angeles Black community, the conference was attended by over 500 labor, community, religious and academic activists from the western U.S. and Mexico. On the last day of the conference, a statewide network was organized, made up of six local plant closure coalitions in California, including the one in Ontario. Called Californians Against Plant Shutdowns (CAL-CAPS), the network was established to share resources and information, and to join forces to promote state plant closures legislation.

At the height of the struggle to keep the plant open, the Plant Closures Project (a labor-religious-community coalition based in Oakland) and the Northern California Interfaith Council on Economic Justice and Work obtained letters of solidarity from GE workers in Mexico, South Korea, Singapore and Brazil—countries where GE's runaway shops have located. This show of international support encouraged the Ontario workers and also reinforced their understanding that their problems were caused by GE and the corporate system, and not by workers in other countries.

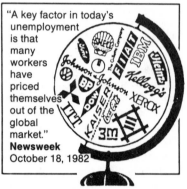

MYTHS AND REALITIES

Between 1978 and 1982, 6.8 million manufacturing jobs were lost as a direct result of plant shutdowns in the United States. [1] One out of every three manufacturing jobs existing in 1978 had disappeared by 1982. The prevailing mythology tells us that workers have "priced themselves out" and that government has taxed and regulated business out of competition in the global market. The mythical solution is to get workers and government "off the backs"

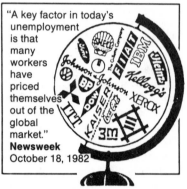

"A key factor in today's unemployment is that many workers have priced themselves out of the global market."
Newsweek
October 18, 1982

of business and let "free enterprise" reign with lower wages, lower taxes and little regulation.

Blame It On Wages

Of all the common misconceptions about plant closures, none is more insidious than that which puts the blame on allegedly "overpaid" workers. Once a source of national pride, a middle income wage for blue collar work is now taken as a sign of greed and decadence. The image is that workers' wages have been rising steadily, giving U.S. business a disadvantage in international competition. In fact, real U.S. wages, adjusted for inflation, have *declined* significantly since their postwar peak in 1972. As the chart shows, there was a 16 percent fall in real wages between 1972 and 1982. According to The Institute for Labor Education and Research, "The country's gross national product (GNP) more than doubled during the 1970's, but *the standard of living provided by the average worker's earnings was lower in 1981 than it was in 1956.*" Corporate executives, meanwhile, fared much better: the average earnings in a sample of about 500 top corporate executives rose by 18 percent, accounting for inflation, between 1976 and 1979. [2]

In the auto industry, much has been made of the supposedly large difference in U.S. and Japanese wages—as if wages and not other factors, such as Japanese plant modernization and speed-up, were behind the lower cost of producing a standard automobile in Japan. In dollar amounts, U.S. workers do not make much more than Japanese when bonuses and overtime are included, and they make substantially less in such non-wage benefits as subsidized housing, national health insurance and job security. Buried in the stampede to scapegoat workers for the decline of the American auto industry is the huge salary gap found at management levels. In 1978, Toyota's top 34 executives were paid $43.90 per hour, while General Motors' top 55 executives were making $263.54 per hour—a difference of $219.64 per hour![3]

Overall, U.S. manufacturing workers are not the world's most highly paid. By 1979, U.S. workers in manufacturing made less than comparable workers in six European countries: West Germany, Sweden, the Netherlands, Belgium, Denmark and Switzerland. And contrary to prevailing mythology, the U.S. does not have the world's highest standard of living. In a 1983 social-economic ranking of countries based upon per-capita Gross National Product, health and education data, the United States was tied for ninth with Belgium, behind first-ranked Sweden, Norway, Denmark, France, Iceland, West Germany, Australia and Finland.[4]

The United States compares unfavorably with Western Europe and Japan in a wide range of economic and social areas. In data for the mid-

Gross Average Weekly Earnings of Private Sector Non-Agricultural Workers 1972—1982

"The standard of living of the average American has to decline."
— Paul Volcker
Federal Reserve Board Chairman
1979

Adjusted for Inflation

1972	$198.41
1973	$198.35
1974	$190.12
1975	$184.16
1976	$186.65
1977	$189.00
1978	$189.31
1979	$183.41
1980	$172.74
1981	$170.13
1982	$167.87

Steve Cagan

Source: U.S. Bureau of Labor Statistics
Handbook of Labor Statistics, 1983.

and late-1970s, compiled by Ira Magaziner and Robert Reich,[5] the U.S. ranks:

* most unequal in distribution of wealth;
* last in social welfare expenditures as a percentage of Gross National Product;
* last in workers' average paid vacations;
* only country without national health insurance;
* highest infant mortality rate;
* last in percentage of unemployed workers covered by unemployment insurance and last in unemployment benefits as a percentage of average earnings;
* worst in air pollution;
* highest homicide rate.

Not surprisingly, the U.S. is also last when it comes to union membership as a percentage of total wage and salary earnings. In 1978, when Sweden, Belgium, West Germany and Britain had union memberships ranging from 83 percent to 55 percent, the U.S. rate was 21 percent.[6] Today the U.S. rate is around 15 percent. It is precisely because wages and benefits are generally higher in unionized firms, and because unions are strong advocates of social welfare benefits, that Corporate America is so intent upon weakening trade unions even further. The corporate view is clearly stated in the box on page 16, with excerpts from a report by the highly respected Business International Corporation, written in 1980, before the Reagan round of government cutbacks, deregulation, union-busting and worker concessions.

Who Needs to Make Wage Concessions?

U.S.—Japanese Auto Industry

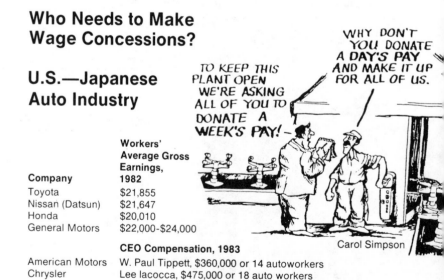

Company	Workers' Average Gross Earnings, 1982
Toyota	$21,855
Nissan (Datsun)	$21,647
Honda	$20,010
General Motors	$22,000-$24,000

CEO Compensation, 1983

American Motors	W. Paul Tippett, $360,000 or 14 autoworkers
Chrysler	Lee Iacocca, $475,000 or 18 auto workers
Ford	Philip Caldwell, $1,400,000 or 52 autoworkers
General Motors	Roger B. Smith, $1,490,000 or 56 autoworkers

Carol Simpson

Sources: Workers' Policy Project, **It's Time for Management Concessions**, New York, 1982; "Executive Compensation Scoreboard," **Business Week**, May 7, 1984; UAW International Research Department, Detroit.

The Myth of High Corporate Taxes

Although corporations frequently complain about high taxes, the corporate share of federal tax revenues has actually dropped, from around 28 percent in the 1950s to 12 percent in 1980. Arguing that generous tax breaks to business and the wealthy would spur investment and create jobs, the Reagan Administration enacted the "Economic Recovery Tax Act" of 1981. By 1982, the corporate share of the nation's tax burden had fallen to 7.5 percent, while business investment in plants and equipment *declined* by about 7 percent.[7] According to the Center on Budget and Policy Priorities, "the average annual rate of growth in business investment under the Reagan Administration is 4 percent—far below the 15 percent average annual growth rate under the Carter Administration." By 1983, corporate taxes provided just 6 percent of federal revenues. But what about the competition? "Japan—with an economy one-third the size of ours—now collects more in corporate income taxes than the U.S. does."[8]

Corporations have a variety of ways to reduce their tax liabilities and even earn refunds. General Electric provides one example. The GE Credit Corporation (GECC) was established during the Depression to help finance the sale of GE appliances. Today, GECC is a large, diversified financial institution and its major operation is a leasing business, which buys and rents out such diverse equipment as railcars, aircraft and computers. By investing in this equipment, GECC acquires tax credits, which can be used to reduce GE's overall tax bill. In 1982, GE earned a profit of $1.6 billion, for which it was liable for $422 million in federal income taxes. But GECC had accumulated so many tax credits that it not only eliminated GE's entire tax liability, but enabled GE to apply for a tax refund of $176 million.[9]

As the corporate share of U.S. taxes has dropped, the personal income tax system has become more unfair. Low and middle income taxpayers are paying more, while wealthy taxpayers are paying less. Between 1978 and 1981, the effective income tax rate for the bottom half of the population *increased* by over 50 percent, while the taxes paid by those making over $200,000 per year *decreased* by 16 percent.[10] What about Reagan's so-called "across-the-board" tax cut passed in 1981? The Joint Congressional Committee on Taxation has found that the wealthiest 5.6 percent of all taxpayers received 35 percent of the benefits from the tax cut. During the 1983-85 period, taxpayers with incomes over $80,000—the richest 1.5 percent of all Americans—gained, on average, over $24,000. Those earning over $200,000 received a windfall of $60,000. Meanwhile, those with incomes below $10,000 suffered an average loss of $1,100 through the combined effect of budget and tax policies. In short, these policies have added up to billions of dollars in giveaways to corporations and the rich: In the 1981-83 period, households earning under $20,000 lost an estimated total of $19.7 billion, while households earning over $80,000 gained $34.9 billion.[11]

The American Business Climate Sunny Side Up

"Foreign investment in the US has increased dramatically in the past decade due to the relatively low wages (in 1979, the US ranked seventh in wage rates among industrialized nations) and to the absence of laws on industrial democracy and worker layoffs, which severely restrict management flexibility and increase costs in Europe...

"On the positive side, employers point to the long-term trend toward decreased union power in political affairs—as indicated by the defeat in 1978 of a union-backed labor-reform bill—and the loss of union members in the past decade. Employers also note a marked success in programs designed to increase productivity and maintain a union-free operation, including quality-of-working life programs and productivity incentive plans (called Scanlon plans). Several industries—notably the steel and automotive industries, which have witnessed large declines in employment—have also witnessed an increasingly cooperative union attitude, resulting in joint management-union programs designed to increase productivity and competitiveness...

"Following the burst of reforms in industrial relations and social welfare during the 1960s, the past decade has been characterized by increased concern with the cost of social welfare programs and a strong anti-labor tilt in the legislative and executive branches of the US Government...The results have been: the defeat of several measures backed by labor; a shift in Washington from employment and social welfare programs to programs designed to curb inflation, labor costs and the decline in industrial productivity; and business initiatives to curb government regulations in the field of health and safety and other areas.

"Despite the overall trend, union pressure and policies adopted by government regulatory agencies may lead to increased government regulation in some areas, thus increasing business expenses and decreasing company flexibility. Among the areas in which new government initiatives are feared are: health and safety, equal employment opportunity, plant closures, and social security and pension programs.
—Business International Corporate Public Policy Research, **Labor and the Multinational Corporation in the 1980s,** Volume One, New York, 1980.

Too Much Government Regulation ?

Since the 1960s regulatory agencies such as the Occupational Safety and Health Administration (OSHA) and the Environmental Protection Agency (EPA) have established and partially enforced some minimum standards of safety, health and environmental quality. Corporations and the Reagan Administration charge that these regulations cost too much and cause plant closures. The American people, it seems, have to choose between their jobs and their health.

Between six and eight million Americans are injured on the job every year. This figure includes 2.5 million workers who are disabled and 14,000 who are killed at work.[12] Past regulations have been effective in reducing risk. Improved mine inspections and safety rules, for example, contributed to a 75 percent decrease in coal and mine fatalities between 1960 and 1978. Under the Reagan Administration, mine inspections have dropped and fatalities have increased.

According to the National Institute for Occupational Safety and Health (NIOSH), 100,000 people die each year from job related diseases. For example, over 1.5 million American workers inhale arsenic at work every day. These workers are dying of lung and lymphatic cancer at a rate two to eight times higher than the national average. Of the 4 million workers who were heavily exposed to asbestos since World War II, at least 1.6 million will die of asbestos related cancer. Moreover, the hazards of toxic substances spill out into the community. The spouses and children of asbestos workers have died of cancer due to exposure to asbestos carried home on work clothes, and so have community residents who lived near the plant.[13]

Although corporations complain that regulations are sending them to the poorhouse, their behavior proves otherwise. According to a study by the Conservation Foundation, government regulations have virtually no impact on where corporations decide to locate their plants. Regulations have a negligible impact on prices and may have a positive impact on employment. For example, in 1979, pollution control added only two-tenths of one percent to consumer prices, according to a study by Data Resources, Inc. The National Academy of Sciences found that by 1974, pollution control legislation alone had created 677,900 jobs. And, according to EPA estimates, 220,000 jobs have been created in the last decade as a result of clean water requirements.[14]

As mentioned before, the U.S. has the highest level of air pollution among industrialized nations. In the case of the steel industry, according to Magaziner and Reich, the Japanese spent more on pollution control than the U.S. industry, both in absolute terms and as a percentage of total investment. "Pollution and safety levels in Japanese mills are on average far superior."[15] The discovery of increasing health hazards in the workplace and the environment indicates a need for more regulation, not less.

⓷

HAVE PLANTS, WILL TRAVEL

"We take the labor-intensive parts of the unit and manufacture that overseas. The technology-intensive parts are manufactured here in the U.S. The great bulk of the labor is done over there. We set up our company a little different than others. A lot of them began manufacturing here and then moved some operations offshore. We started the company with overseas operations."
Richard DuBridge,
Televideo Vice President[1]

Lynn Duggan

The term "foreign competition" can be misleading in a world in which capital is increasingly internationalized. Between 1950 and 1980, direct foreign investment by U.S. corporations increased sixteen times, from about $12 billion to $192 billion. By the late 1970s, at least one-third—and in many cases the major share—of the overall profits of the 100 largest U.S. corporations and banks came from operations outside the United States.[2] The U.S. economy is dominated by these *multinational corporations* which have operations strategically located in many countries. Today, "about 70 percent of manufacturing income in the United States and other major industrial countries is earned by multinational companies that have branches, subsidiaries, or joint ventures outside their 'home' country."[3] Take the auto industry. After failing to meet consumer preferences for smaller, fuel-efficient cars, U.S. auto companies closed plant after plant, citing Japanese competition as the cause. But the lines between the Japanese and U.S. auto industry are increasingly blurred. According to 1983 data, Ford owns 25 percent of the

Japanese firm, Toyo Kogyo (makers of Mazda), which provides Ford with engines and manual transaxles. GM owns 34.4 percent of Izuzu motors which provides GM with engines and transmissions for mini-trucks, Chevettes, S-cars and J-cars. Chrysler owns 15 percent of Mitsubishi Motors, which builds the Dodge Ram 50.[4] In 1984, GM formed a joint venture with Toyota to produce a subcompact car at the site of its recently closed plant in Fremont, California.

The multinational corporation thrives on "communications technology which can send information at the speed of light and transportation technology which can move at the speed of sound."[5] The world headquarters of the Ford Motor company in Dearborn, Michigan contains rows of IBM computers which feed into every factory that Ford owns around the world. Ford technicians can change the speed of an assembly line in Australia as easily as they can adjust speed in a plant across the street.

Like other corporations, Ford has put advanced technology to work in undermining union leverage by maximizing its ability to pit workers in different factories against each other and minimizing its vulnerability to strikes. Ford's "world cars" apply the strategies of *parallel production*, producing identical products in plants in different locations, and *outsourcing*, subcontracting to multiple suppliers. The Ford *Escort* uses parts, plants and assembly operations in 15 countries outside the U.S., including Austria, Belgium, Canada, England, France, Italy, Japan, Northern Ireland, Spain and West Germany.[6]

U.S. banks play a key role in the redeployment of industrial assets around the world. A case in point is the highly publicized shutdown of Ohio's Youngstown Sheet and Tube Company, owned by the Lykes Corporation since 1969. Barry Bluestone and Bennett Harrison observe that in the mid-1970s, three of Lyke's principal bankers began withdrawing financial support, needed for modernization, while increasing investments in the Japanese Steel industry. Between 1975 and 1977, Citibank increased loans to Japan from $59 million to $230 million, Chase Manhattan Bank from $59 million to $204 million, and Chemical Bank from $15 million to over $82 million. Chase and Citicorp also invested heavily in the state-owned South African Iron and Steel Corporation (ISCOR). They provided almost 90 percent of ISCOR's $538 million in U.S. bank loans between 1972 and 1978. The major foreign customers for ISCOR's iron ore and other minerals were the "same Japanese steelmakers who had received such enormous loans from the very U.S. banks that were disinvesting in Youngstown," say Bluestone and Harrison. "Finally, to complete the circle, in 1979, according to U.S. Department of Commerce records, ISCOR's rapid growth made South Africa the fifth most important exporter of processed iron and steel to the United States." Meanwhile, the U.S. Steel Corporation was complaining loudly about "foreign competition" while also investing in South Africa. In its 1979 annual report it lists partial ownership of four South African mining and mineral processing enterprises, with shares ranging from 20 to 49 percent.[7]

Under the apartheid system, the passbook has been used to regulate Black labor and control the movements of Black South Africans.

Investing In Apartheid Steel

"Although most foreign steel comes from Europe and Japan, a growing percentage is from low-wage Third World countries such as Brazil, and South Africa. In January 1984, Third World steel accounted for 10.1 percent of the U.S. market...Since 1975 U.S. imports of South African steel have increased 5,000 percent!...

"The main reason why South African steel can compete with U.S.-produced steel is South Africa's labor control system known as apartheid... Five of every six South Africans are black. Yet: they cannot live or work where they choose; they risk jail if they strike for better wages or justice on the job; they have no say in the government that rules them—they are not allowed to vote...

"Most South African steel is produced by the government-owned Iron and Steel Corporation (ISCOR). ISCOR plays a vital role in the South African economy and the government has provided it with numerous subsidies, cheap raw materials, low-wage black labor, financing, transportation, tax breaks, and import barriers to keep foreign competition out of the South African market...

"ISCOR could not have grown to its present large size without the help of U.S. corporations and banks. Companies such as U.S. Steel, ARMCO, Phelps Dodge, Allegheny Ludlum, and Standard Pressed Steel Co., have pumped billions of dollars worth of capital and technology into South Africa for decades. Among the U.S. banks that have loaned hundreds of millions of dollars to ISCOR are Chase Manhattan, Citicorp, Continental Illinois, Kidder Peabody, First Boston, Merrill Lynch, Smith Barney, Manufacturers Hanover, and Morgan Guarantee Trust...

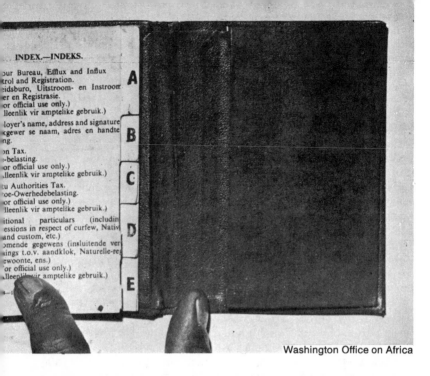

INDEX.—INDEKS.

our Bureau, Efflux and Influx
trol and Registration.
idsburo, Uitstroom- en Instroom
er en Registrasie.
or official use only.)
lleenlik vir amptelike gebruik.)

loyer's name, address and signature
gewer se naam, adres en handte
ng.

on Tax.
-belasting.
or official use only.)
lleenlik vir amptelike gebruik.)

tu Authorities Tax.
oe-Owerhedebelasting.
or official use only.)
lleenlik vir amptelike gebruik.)

itional particulars (includin
essions in respect of curfew, Nativ
and custom, etc.)
omende gegewens (insluitende ver
ings t.o.v. aandklok, Naturelle-re
ewoonte, ens.)
or official use only.)
lleenlik vir amptelike gebruik.)

Washington Office on Africa

"Chicago steelworkers discovered that steel beams being used to construct a new state building in their city were imported from South Africa. At the same time, U.S. Steel's Southworks plant in Chicago—which makes the same kind of steel beams—had laid off steelworkers by the thousands. Meanwhile, Continental Illinois, a bank in the Chicago area, was loaning money to South Africa's steel company, ISCOR, that made the beams...

"Workers at Phelps Dodge copper mines in Arizona, on strike since July 1983 for better wages and working conditions, have been met with brutal force by the company and state police. The company refuses to negotiate with the workers' unions, insisting on wage concessions. The corporation has laid off hundreds of workers in the last year, citing 'foreign competition.' Yet Phelps Dodge is the seventh largest U.S. investor in South Africa, taking full advantage of apartheid labor repression. At its fluorspar mine, Africans earn less than 40 cents an hour, working 60 hours a week in 26 ten-hour shifts a month and sleeping 12 to a room in migrant labor hostels...

"By working to force these companies out of South Africa we can assist the struggle for democracy in South Africa, while strengthening the U.S. economy at the same time...Imposing economic sanctions on South Africa and divesting American pension funds from companies profiting from apartheid will benefit both the black majority of South Africa and American workers..."

Excerpted from: **American Steel Jobs and South Africa**   A publication of the United Steelworkers of America and the Washington Office on Africa Educational Fund, September 1984.

They'd Rather Be Merging

"There is nothing written in the sky that says the world would not be a perfectly satisfactory place if there were only 100 companies."
William Baxter, Reagan Administration's first Anti-Trust chief

Profits have always made the business world go round, but a new breed of corporate money managers has been foregoing longterm productive investments for the sake of higher short-term profit margins. Often, they find more money to be made in mergers and speculation—real estate, commodities, international currencies—than in new production. *Forbes* magazine reports, "It wasn't long ago that buying something for a billion dollars made you distinctive...Ten-digit deals weren't common until the 1980s, with Reaganomics and the 1981 tax law in full swing and antitrust enforcement in full retreat." Increasingly, says *Forbes*, "businesses become mere commodities for trading in the marketplace as casually as a sack of sugar or a suburban house. If your business is a troubled one, don't break your back dealing with the problems, just trade it in for a different model."[8] And, if it's not troubled, trade it in anyway for a model with bigger profits.

Two out of three "new" manufacturing plants which were added to the rolls of *Fortune* 500 company holdings between 1972 and 1980 were not new at all, but simply purchased from another company.[9] In 1983, corporations spent $73.1 billion in 2,533 mergers.[10] That same year, according to *Business Week*, "less than $1 billion in venture capital was allocated from private funds and corporations with venture capital subsidiaries." As one corporate officer puts it, "It's the defunding of America."[11]

Modern conglomerates often establish a minimum rate of profit called a "hurdle rate" for all of their holdings. Hurdle rates commonly average between 25 percent and 40 percent return on investment.[12] Reinvestment is essential to the maintenance of healthy industries, but it can take years to pay off. Instead of reinvesting in a plant that is making profit below the company's hurdle rate, executives increasingly choose to sell it or shut it down, and then acquire some other business which is already bringing in the acceptable rate of profit.

In some cases, a profitable company may be purchased as a convenient source of cash to finance a conglomerate's speculative ventures. Corporations call these acquisitions "cash cows" because they are "milked" for their profits to subsidize other investments. Without funds for reinvestment, the "cash cow" may start to lose money, and then be shut down by the new owner "because it is no longer profitable." Workers often become the scapegoats for these self-fulfilling prophecies of declining profits.

U.S. Steel, long the world's dominant steelmaker, provides a good example of the devastating impact of disinvestment in production facilities. By the 1970s, "Big Steel" had earned a reputation as a museum piece, with the oldest plants in the industry: "their 'newest' integrated steel mill was built in 1953, and their major mills at Gary, Indiana and

Fairfield, Alabama, were constructed at the turn of the century."[13] Between 1976 and 1979, almost half of U.S. Steel's new profits were invested in non-steel activities, including plastics, chemicals, a shopping mall and a Disney World hotel.[14] Still, the conglomerate's steel production remained profitable, bringing in a 6.7 percent return on the dollar, a rate higher than other steel companies, but far lower than the profits of U.S. Steel's other ventures at 20 percent and up. These high profit ventures attracted increasing amounts of the company's capital, so that today, U.S. Steel has under 25 percent of its assets in the steel industry.[15]

With growing competition from modernized plants in Japan and elsewhere, U.S. Steel began to report losses in its steel holdings. Since 1979, when David M. Roderick took over as chairman, U.S. Steel has shut down more than 150 plants and facilities, reducing steelmaking capacity by more than 30 percent.[16] In 1980, the company employed 171,654 people. By 1984, only 80,000 remained employed.[17] In the early 1980s, U.S. Steel demanded wage concessions from steelworkers and tax concessions from taxpayers in order to "save the industry." The Reagan Administration's 1981 "Economic Recovery Act" gave the company a tax break of $850 million, with the purpose of stimulating investment in plants and equipment.[18] In 1983, with layoffs mounting, the steelworkers invested deeper in the future of the industry by accepting a $250 per month cut in pay, totaling $3 billion dollars.[19]

But at every turn, Big Steel sold out its workers and U.S. taxpayers by continuing its disinvestment in steel. In 1982, the company spent $6.6 billion to purchase Marathon Oil in the second biggest merger in corporate history. Today, U.S. Steel is seeking another massive acquisi-

Steve Cagan

tion to form a "third leg" outside both steel and oil. Chairman Roderick, says *Business Week*, is considering changing the corporate name. Earlier, in response to protests by steelworkers angered at the company's betrayal of their concessions, Roderick asserted, "U.S. Steel is not in the business of making steel. It is in the business of making money."[20]

Legal Hostages

Capital mobility is a powerful instrument of blackmail which corporations use to exact tribute from state and local governments as well as workers. Cities and states are locked in a fierce competition to keep old industries and win new ones. The way to "win" in this competition is by offering lower wages and better tax incentives, public facilities and financing, and other forms of corporate welfare and legal bribery. A State of Michigan advertisement pictures a business executive pointing a gun to his head; his desk is covered with Pennsylvania state tax forms. The caption reads: "Two things in life are certain, death and taxes. At least in Michigan the taxes won't kill you."[21]

Other states boast of so-called "Right-to-Work" laws which create obstacles to union organizing and help ensure low pay scales. "Labor-management relations are excellent...Wage rates are considerably below those found in major manufacturing areas," boasts an Oklahoma brochure called "Profitable Oklahoma." North Carolina has a Right-to-Work promotional brochure highlighting the policies under which its manufacturing workers earn some 30 percent less than the national average.[22]

Bidding wars between the states cause plant closures for some and lower wages and tax revenues for all. In his book on these regional wars, Robert Goodman observes: "This kind of public entrepreneuring...has turned free enterprise on its head, leaving government in the role of competitor and business as welfare recipient. It is a process in which the public takes enormous financial risks, while business surveys the willing suitors and moves freely to where the public risk-taking is greatest."[23]

When GM announced that it would close its last Detroit auto plant, the company told city officials it might consider locating a *new* assembly plant in Detroit (rather than Montgomery, Alabama) under certain conditions. In exchange for the plant and its promised 6,000 jobs, the city was to prepare a specific site in the center of Detroit, known as Poletown, and provide generous tax breaks. Despite organized community opposition, the city agreed to spend tax dollars to relocate two freeway ramps for the GM site and give the company a twelve-year, 50 percent tax abatement which could cost up to $240 million in lost revenues. In 1981, the city used the power of eminent domain to clear over 400 acres, destroying residential neighborhoods and displacing 3,200 people and 160 community businesses.[24] (As of Fall 1985, the plant was partly operational, employing about 3,000 workers, according to GM; a workforce of 5,000 is projected when the plant moves to two shifts.)

Even after all the community sacrifice to attract a new business, there is no assurance that the company will *stay*.

Steve Cagan

Welcome to...
CLEVELAND'S
MODEL CITIES
NEIGHBORHOOD
AIR FORCE
a golden opportunity
CALL (216) 382-8300

Corporate Resettlement, Care of Uncle Sam

The U.S. government subsidizes foreign investment and encourages runaway plants. For example, under existing federal tax law, U.S. corporations need not pay taxes on their foreign profits so long as they are reinvested abroad. In 1972, U.S. corporations earned over $24 billion abroad, but with the help of various tax breaks, they had to pay $1.2 billion in taxes—a rate of only 5 percent.[25] Subcontracting assembly work to low-wage operations in other countries has become increasingly popular, due, in part, to special tax incentives. When the assembled product is imported back into the U.S., the company only has to pay tariffs on the value that was added to the product abroad. The Overseas Private Investment Corporation (OPIC) provides U.S. companies with insurance against war, revolution or expropriation. The U.S. government also helps multinational corporations and their "host" governments through the Export-Import Bank and the Agency for International Development (AID).

U.S. foreign policy is heavily oriented toward protecting the interests of U.S. corporations in their low-wage havens around the world. Take the case of Central America where there are over 1,400 U.S.-owned businesses. In 1980, U.S. direct investment in the region totalled $4.2 billion. That year, when the average U.S. hourly manufacturing wage was $8.76, employees of U.S. affiliates in Central America earned an average wage of only $1.08.[26]

A 1981 Rand Corporation report, prepared for the U.S. Commerce Department, portrayed El Salvador as the perfect fiefdom for U.S. business:

[El Salvador's] greatest advantage lies in the character of the working people, who are industrious, adapt willingly to new methods, and demand lower wages than those prevailing in the developed world. It is said that if you tell Salvadorans to plant rocks and harvest more rocks, they'll do it...[27]

In the late 1960s El Salvador improved its accommodations for U.S. industry with the opening of the San Bartolo Free Trade Zone, just outside the capital of San Salvador. Like Free Trade Zones elsewhere in the Third World, the San Bartolo Zone offered cheap labor under repressive conditions. With the 1974 Export Promotion Law, El Salvador competed more agressively for U.S. plants. The law permitted total tax exemptions on imports of machinery, equipment and spare parts; a ten-year reprieve from income and capital gains tax; unrestricted repatriation of profits to the U.S.; and a special employment agency to recruit labor. U.S. companies moved to El Salvador, often running away

Women and the Global Assembly Line Project

from *other Third World countries*. Dataram, an electronics company, opened up in El Salvador after closing shop in Malaysia. Texas Instruments moved in after shutting down its plant in Curacao.[28] In 1984, Texas Instruments was El Salvador's largest U.S. employer. Except for supervisors and top management all 2,400 employees are women— the cheapest of cheap labor—assembling components for pocket calculators and digital watches.

The same oppressive economic and political conditions which have made Central America such a bargain for U.S. agribusiness and industrial corporations, fostered dissent among Central American peasants and workers. In 1979, Nicaragua changed the course of it's destiny as a cheap labor haven, with the Sandinista-led revolution. The Reagan Administration has been trying to economically and militarily destabilize the Nicaraguan Government, the first democratically-elected government in that country after four decades of Somoza family dictatorships. As the revolutionary war in El Salvador heated up in the early 1980s—after non-violent opposition was crushed—many U.S. companies pulled out American personnel, leaving Salvadorans in charge; others pulled out altogether. According to the *New York Times* of March 24, 1984, the Texas Instrument plant is guarded by a security force headed by a retired Salvadoran army major. The U.S. Government is pouring increasing amounts of military and economic aid into El Salvador to defeat the popular revolution and recreate a hospitable climate for U.S. business—where Salvadorans will industriously "plant rocks" at the behest of American bosses.

Another case in point is the Philippines, a former U.S. colony where U.S. multinationals have had strong economic influence. In 1972 President Marcos declared martial law and the U.S. responded by doubling its loans and military aid to the Philippines to assure that Marcos could "stabilize" the country and protect U.S. investments. Marcos issued orders which denied workers the right to strike, imposed restrictions on union organizing and eliminated the minimum wage requirement of *$3.93 per day* for foreign owned companies, established Free Trade Zones (called Export Processing Zones in the Philippines), eliminated tariffs and permitted polluting industries to operate in the country without restriction. With the help of U.S. economic advisors, the Marcos government restructured economic policy.[29]

By 1979, wages in the Philippines had dropped approximately 30 percent below 1972 levels, to 49 cents an hour. The Philippines had become the cheapest source of labor in Asia, attracting U.S. runaways that had previously located in other countries, such as Singapore where 1979 wages were 95 cents per hour, Taiwan where wages were 85 cents an hour and Hong Kong, where workers were paid $1.41 per hour.[30] In the Philippines today, there is vigorous, growing opposition to the Marcos dictatorship.

U.S. Government policies which encourage runaway investment and aid repressive "host" regimes are detrimental to the rights of all working people—in the United States and abroad.

WELCOME TO THE CORPORATE FUTURE

The business community and their White House allies try to soothe the ache of unemployment and economic upheaval by claiming that our problems will soon be over. They say the United States is simply experiencing the growing pains of a post-industrial revolution, where old industries, like auto, steel and textiles are being replaced by "high tech" manufacturing and a new service economy. In their view, the Rustbowl sweeping the industrial heartland is the price of economic progress; in due time, there will be jobs enough to go around in the new economy.

But when we look behind the rhetoric, we can see that plant closures are part of a trend which has been called "the disappearing middle," a growing polarization between large numbers of low-wage, low-skilled jobs and a small number of highly paid professional, managerial and technical jobs. A 1984 study by Barry Bluestone, Bennett Harrison and Lucy Gorham shows that the occupations which will produce the most jobs over the next 10 years, concentrated in the service sector, paid an average wage below $12,500 in 1980. (See chart below.) The manufacturing occupations providing fewer jobs for the future paid average wages above $22,000 in 1980. These jobs are located in unionized industries like auto and basic steel which have been hardest hit by plant closures.[1]

Unionization rates in the manufacturing sector were relatively high, at 36.9 percent for men and 22.2 percent for women in 1980. But waves of plant closures have decimated union ranks. Between 1976 and 1983 membership in the United Steelworkers of America fell a staggering 47.3 percent; the International Association of Machinists lost 38.7 percent; and the United Auto Workers lost 23.6 percent.[2] New manufacturing jobs in high-tech industries are largely non-unionized and pay significantly lower wages than the unionized older industries.

Occupations Producing Most New Jobs

Bill Day

	1980 Employment	% Growth 1980-1990	Women's 1981 Median Weekly Wage
*Secretaries	2,469,000	28.3	$229
*Nurses' Aides, Orderlies	1,175,000	43.2	$167
Janitors, Sextons	2,751,000	18.2	$188
Sales Clerks	2,880,000	16.7	$154
*Cashiers	1,597,000	28.4	$166
*Professional Nurses	1,104,000	39.6	$331
Truck Drivers	1,696,000	24.5	N.A.
*Fast Food Workers	**806,000**	**49.6**	**$140**
*General Office Clerks	2,395,000	15.8	$222
*Waiters, Waitresses	1,711,000	21.1	$144
*Elementary Teachers	1,286,000	19.5	$311
Kitchen Helpers	839,000	27.6	$160
Accountants, Auditors	833,000	26.5	$308
Construction Helpers	955,000	22.2	$252
Automotive Mechanics	846,000	24.4	$286

*Percent of women in job category over 80 percent.

Source: Bureau of Labor Statistics figures, cited in **New York Times**, October 16, 1983; Weekly wage figures compiled by Prof. Teresa Amott, Women for Economic Justice, Boston, MA.

In 1948, about one in every three American jobs was in manufacturing. In 1984, manufacturing's share of total employment was below 22 percent, down from 29 percent in 1968; during this same period, services' share of the private sector workforce rose from 54 percent to about 64 percent.[3] The Bureau of Labor Statistics predicts that services will account for 75 percent of all new jobs created between 1982 and 1995.[4]

A 1984 survey of workers laid off from the U.S. Steel Corporation's Chicago South Works (undertaken by The Hull House Association of

Chicago and Local 65 of the United Steelworkers of America) illustrates the dramatic income gap between old job and new job. As reported by the *New York Times*, on October 31, 1984, "The average income of workers laid off...in the last five years has been cut almost in half...the laid-off workers, whose household income averaged $22,000 a year in 1979, had a median household income of about $12,500 in 1983." One of the survey respondents wrote, "To go from earning $20,000 plus to being at an employer's mercy for $3.35 an hour is devastating." The survey also found:

11 percent [of the respondents] said they had been evicted and 38 percent said they had fallen behind in mortgage or rent payments.
   Seventeen percent of the laid-off workers said they received welfare assistance for some period after losing their jobs and 35 percent said they received food stamps. Two-fifths said they had no health insurance and three-fourths said they had put off receiving health care at some point because of lost insurance.

"For every manufacturing job lost we need to create two to three jobs in the service sector," says Barry Bluestone, who explains that to maintain a middle-class income in the future, several family members will have to work at the available lower-paying jobs.[5] Understood in this light, the growth in women's employment outside the home is less a mark of progress than a measure of the decline in real wages outside the traditionally low-wage Pink Collar women's job ghetto. And, for the growing numbers of women-headed households—now over 15 percent of all households—the shortage of decent wages is devastating.

Bursting The High Tech Bubble

Contrary to its media image, the promise of booming high-tech employment is an empty one. Ronald Kutscher, Assistant Commissioner of the Bureau of Labor Statistics reports that, "High-tech industries, even broadly defined, will account for only a small proportion of new jobs through 1995."[6] Furthermore, the majority of "high-tech" workers are not Yuppie computer wizards, but low-paid assembly workers whose average wage in 1980 was $4.52 per hour.[7] Most of these workers do not belong to unions. When the American Electronics Association surveyed its 1,900 member companies in 1982, less than 5 percent reported having any unionized workers.[8] In part to preserve these low rates of pay and unionization, the high-tech sector is undergoing its own wave of layoffs and plant closures.

Just a few years ago, "Atari" was not only a successful maker of home computers and video games, it was another name for high tech: as in "Atari Democrats." On February 22, 1983, Atari announced that it

AFSC Nationwide Womens' Program

was laying off 1,700 employees, a quarter of its U.S. workforce, and shifting production to Hong Kong. The first 600 workers to be laid off received *one day's notice.* The Atari layoff shocked and angered high-tech advocates and public officials across the country. The Alabama legislature called the move a "Judas decision" and demanded a national boycott of all Atari products.[9]

Atari's runaway occurred right in the middle of a union organizing drive by the Glaziers and Glass Workers Union. According to union organizer Ed Jones, Atari's move to Asia will only save the company 3 to 4 percent on existing costs. Jones believes that the real reason Atari laid off its 1,700 workers was to thwart present and future attempts to organize high-tech assembly workers into unions. "What you see is a definite trend," says Jones, "dividing tasks between the high-tech worker in the states—research and development, engineering, and that type of thing. And then they're shifting the blue collar work overseas."[10]

A 1984 study of the high-tech industry in Silicon Valley and throughout California showed that nearly 43,000 high-tech workers lost their jobs in 147 closures and layoffs between January 1980 and January 1984.[11]

Losing Ground

Women and minorities are being disproportionately affected by the layoffs and shutdowns in both basic manufacturing and high-tech. When Atari shut down its California plant, 80 percent of the workers laid off were Latino/a and Asian. When GE reduced its U.S. workforce by 28,000 in 1982, including the 1,000 Ontario workers, the total proportion of minorities employed by GE dropped by 1 percent. Acknowledging the problem, but not its cause, GE spokesperson Larry Vaber comments, "the recession has slowed our company's progress in equal opportunity for minorities and women."[12]

Minority workers are heavily concentrated in the regions, occupations and industries which have been swept by plant closures. The auto industry provides a striking example. In 1980, when 18 percent of the auto workforce was on layoff, almost 32 percent of the industry's Black workers were unemployed. According to the UAW'S civil rights department, layoffs in the auto industry alone were responsible for a 1 percent drop in the 1983 national average income for Blacks.[13] Black teenagers are finding little or no opportunities for employment. In 1982, when unemployment for U.S. teenagers was 21 percent, it was 28 percent for Latino youth and 50 percent for Black teenagers.[14] In an auto town like Detroit, where overall unemployment was 23 percent in 1982, unemployment was 38 percent for all teenagers and a staggering 70 percent for Black youth.[15] In October 1985, the national unemployment rate was 7 percent overall and 15 percent for Blacks.

Women have been hard hit with layoffs in largely female assembly lines, such as textiles, and in the higher paid blue collar jobs which affirmative action helped open up. Elizabeth Stanley worked at the General Motors plant in Fremont, California for almost 10 years. The first woman to be elected to her union Local's Executive Board, Stanley was laid off three months before the Fremont plant was closed permanently. Most of the 1,300 women workers who were laid off from the GM plant had less than 10 years seniority and, as a result, most were not eligible for vested pension benefits. Many of them had very little unemployment left, since they had used a lot of it in earlier layoffs which preceded the shutdown. "A lot of the women who had come into the plant had left jobs in basically women's occupations as waitresses or clerks," says Stanley. "They had left these jobs not only because they paid so poorly, but because they had such low status in businesses that were usually run by men. After working for years at GM, a lot of these women had obtained a new sense of independence."[16]

Displaced women workers are twice as likely as men to stay unemployed for longer than a year, after a plant closure.[17] In the U.S. Steel Chicago South Works case mentioned earlier, the study found that "Minorities and women lost more ground than did whites." While the overall unemployment rate for men was 44 percent, for women it was 63 percent. And while a high number of whites remained unemployed—30 percent—the rates for minority workers were far higher, at 60 percent for Blacks and 47 percent for Latinos.

White Collar Runaways

"The analysts say employers are attracted to the suburbs in part by the pool of white female workers, who the employers see as more malleable and home-oriented than other workers, newer to the job market, less likely to be interested in unionization and more interested in working part time with minimum benefits."
New York Times, October 15, 1984

As the clerical portion of the service economy grows it is attempting to continue the tradition of low pay and benefits that accompany "women's work." As clerical workers begin to organize unions and demand better wages and working conditions, they are finding that their jobs are also vulnerable to runaway shops.

As with manufacturing, technology is eroding the constraints of time and geography in clerical work. Information-processing technology is creating new opportunities for companies to reduce the number of clerical workers needed, downgrade clerical skills and, with the help of electronic communications systems, move clerical work to lower-paying towns and countries (such as Barbados, where women earn about $1.50 an hour) and bust unions. Electronic strike-breaking is possible, as MIT Professor Harley Shaiken explains: "If a picket line is around the home office, work can be processed as easily a hundred miles away or a thousand miles away."[18]

Representative Albert Gore of Tennessee described new innovations in data processing at a 1983 congressional committee meeting:

I recently found out about a project to transfer America's legal precedence onto computer tape. It is one example of many projects that involve the transfer of information stored on ink and paper into the form of electromagnetic digital impulses that can be manipulated in computers. This project by Westlaw, I believe is being carried out in South Korea. They are hiring two women for each law book and are having them input the data. In many cases they do not even read English. Then a computer program automatically matches any differences between the two input streams and highlights them and someone who does read English comes and checks it and corrects it. The end result is error-free computer tapes...which are then transmitted by satellite to the U.S. in less than a second.[19]

More common than the development of international office pools is the tendency for clerical employers to use their increased mobility to bust unions and seek lower-wage regions within the U.S. In April 1981, Blue Shield broke a 15-week strike of Medicare claims processors by transferring 448 jobs from its San Francisco headquarters to outlying areas where unionization is weak.[20]

George Davis, secretary-treasurer of San Francisco's largest white collar union, the Office and Professional Employee's Union Local 3, noted that women and minorities held about 85 percent of the jobs that Blue Shield was moving. "Blue Shield management wants to remove the jobs to communities where unionization and affirmative action pressures are generally non-existent," says Davis.[21] At a 1981 national conference of all Office and Professional Employee Union locals that have contracts with Blue Shield, Davis learned that all of the Blue Shield locals were facing similar problems across the country.

As long as the economy is organized around the sole purpose of maximizing corporate profit, plant closures will continue to occur in factories and offices throughout the country. The hard-won gains of the labor, civil rights and women's movements are being gradually reversed—with reduced wages and job opportunities for *all* workers. We have a lot more to lose. It's time for all of us to fight plant closures.

IT'S TIME TO FIGHT PLANT CLOSURES

Today corporate officers have the right to decide if profitable plants will be shut down, if the United States will maintain a viable steel industry, if profits will be used to create jobs in the U.S. or run away overseas. Workers and communities have no control. We are, however, expected to pay for the social costs of sudden job loss and shoulder more and more of the risks of investment.

We need a new way of thinking about the economy. In the words of Reverend Charles Rawlings of the Ohio Episcopal Diocese: "We have to abandon the 200 year old American Dream that somehow the exercise of selfishness in the form of profitmaking accrues to the benefit of our children and our grandchildren. We've got to kick the habit of thinking that's the way it works."[1]

We can begin to "kick the habit" by observing that corporations are not the only investors in the economy. We are all investors, even if we own no stock in any corporation. As workers, we invest our labor into the production process and pensions into public and private financial institutions. As community members, we pay for the roads and utility lines and other public services which are essential to economic activity, as well as the costs of educating the next generation of workers. As consumers, we purchase the goods and services produced. When the workers at U.S. Steel accepted pay cuts to help save the steel industry, they intended to *invest* their wages in the future of steel. Taxpayers were told they were *investing* in the future of American industry and employment with the "Economic Recovery Act" of 1981. But workers and communities were not consulted and received no dividend checks when U.S. Steel spent billions of dollars to purchase Marathon Oil. Instead, we have been trapped into subsidizing mergers and runaway shops.

It is time for workers and communities to demand the right to participate in economic decisions which affect our lives—decisions which hold the keys to improving or destroying the quality of life and work in the United States. We can't stop plant closures in a piecemeal fashion, defending our plants one by one. We need to build a strong plant closures movement, presenting a broad grassroots challenge to corporate control over our economy and our communities. Jobs with decent wages and working conditions should be a right, not a precarious privilege.

Corporate executives threaten to close their plants to assure that workers and communities will not fight back. But, if the plant closures movement has learned anything, it has learned that corporations are more likely to run away if we *don't* fight back. The more we fight plant closures, the more we learn about how to fight back. Thus, win or lose, every organized campaign against shutdowns has helped advance the movement. There is no all-purpose formula for fighting a closure, because every situation is different and every community has its own unique problems and resources. There are, however, basic elements which are essential to any fightback campaign, described below. Later, we provide concrete examples of fightback strategies which may be modified and used in new situations.

Plant Closures Project

Essential Elements Of Fightback Campaigns

Community-Labor Coalition

Because plant closures affect almost everyone in a community, the single most important weapon against shutdowns is a broad community-labor coalition. Such coalitions have been the backbone of every significant fightback campaign. An organization is the necessary starting point from which to begin building a coalition. The type of organization best situated to organizing a plant closure coalition may vary from community to community. In Ontario, California broad community support for the fight against General Electric was organized by the United Electrical Workers union. In Youngstown, Ohio the first community-labor coalition against plant shutdowns was initiated by leaders of Youngstown's Ecumenical Coalition of church parishes. In

Pittsburgh, Pennsylvania a local community organization, the Bloom-field-Garfield Corporation, provided the initial organizing resources to establish the Save Nabisco Action Coalition, discussed later.

Information

One of the biggest obstacles to fighting shutdowns is that companies give little or no advance warning. A 1983 study, reported in *Business Week* (October 24, 1983), showed that 54 percent of dislocated workers received less than one week's notice of shutdowns. The more time we have before an announced closure occurs, the better we can organize to stop it, develop viable alternative ownership, or, at worst, negotiate a good severance contract, mobilize special services for the unemployed and retrain workers for new jobs. Since corporations have no desire or obligation to let us know their plans, it is essential that workers and community people use alternative methods for acquiring needed information. The following activities can be easily carried out without any special assistance or training:

Early Warning Signs
Of Plant Closures:
A Checklist

1. Your company opens a new plant in another location which produces the same product but pays lower wages.
2. Facilities are run down and buildings are not maintained.
3. Machinery is old and outdated.
4. Hours are cut back, overtime is eliminated and/or temporary layoffs are announced.
5. Your industry has been declining within the last decade.
6. Fewer product lines are manufactured in your plant.
7. Production schedules are irregular.
8. Repairs are not made due to a shortage of machine parts.
9. There is no inventory of spare parts.
10. The research and development department is cut back or transferred.
11. Managers, skilled labor and machinery are shifted to newer plants.
12. Managers are frequently replaced.
13. Advertising of your product is cut back or eliminated; advertisements appear for another version of your product.
14. Productivity standards are increased and older workers who cannot meet them are fired.
15. The outside of your plant has been painted or a new fence erected around the plant.
16. The company will not settle any grievances and makes every problem go to arbitration.

* **Learn the early warning signs** of plant closures and organize an **early warning committee** in your plant to monitor danger signals of an impending shutdown (see boxes).

* **Read business press,** such as your newspaper's business section, business journals and trade magazines to follow trends in your industry and your company. See if your company publishes an **annual report**; it will list corporate income and expenditures, executives and board members, subsidiaries, and future plans.

* **Establish a community watchdog committee,** using the contacts in your community-labor coalition, to develop a broader picture of how closures are affecting your community and gain enough lead time to confront potential future closures.

Media

Corporations spend millions of advertising and promotion dollars to project a positive public image and have free daily coverage in newspaper business sections, written from a management point of view.

How To Organize An
Early Warning Committee

An early warning committee should include **at least one representative from each shift** to monitor employee cutbacks, rumors about the plant, and increased worker harassment which often occurs when management has no future investment in good labor-management relations. The committee should also include **representatives from each of the following departments**:

* **Shipping and Receiving:** They can report if your product is being sent to a new location or if there has been a significant change in what is being shipped and received. They are in constant contact with people whose business is dependent on your plant and are in a position to follow through on those contacts when a fightback campaign is organized.

* **Inventory:** People who work in the storeroom or toolroom can let you know whether normal levels of supplies and machine parts are being ordered or whether stock is significantly low.

* **Maintenance:** They can let you know if maintenance schedules have been changed and if normal maintenance is taking place. They will know if the company is unwilling to spend any money on repairs and asks for make-shift repairs instead, and will also know if the company is doing cosmetic maintenance, e.g., a new paint job to attract buyers and a new fence to keep out workers.

* **Front office:** They have access to management information and should be on the lookout for personnel changes, special inter-office memos which document management decisions, and the hiring of management "consultants," who are often really plant closure specialists.

Government reports also mirror the corporate perspective on the economy. It is essential that fightback campaigns use the media extensively to counter this barrage of corporate propaganda and project alternative points of view. There's a lot more to effective media work than sending out a press release. Work with people in your community knowledgeable about media and public relations to plan a media strategy for your campaign, using a wide variety of publicity techniques: hold press conferences, organize media events with good "photo opportunities," encourage sympathetic public officials and community leaders to speak at your events, meet with editorial boards of local newspapers, write op-ed pieces and letters to the editor, arrange radio interviews, etc.

Your media strategy should generate bad publicity for the company and good publicity for the fightback campaign. As we saw earlier in the Ontario case, bad publicity influenced GE's decision to agree to plant closure language in its national contract with the United Electrical Workers. An effective use of the media will bring your campaign to the broadest possible audience—reaching people who are potential allies and inspiring people to take up their own campaign.

Community Action Against Disinvestment

SNAC Beats Nabisco

In late 1981, Nabisco announced it would close its Pittsburgh plant through a gradual phaseout, giving the Bakers, Confectioners and Tobacco Union about six months to organize an effective fightback campaign. A union member who worked with the Bloomfield-Garfield Corporation, a community organization active in the neighborhood around the plant, asked their assistance in organizing community support. Bloomfield-Garfield donated an organizer, who initiated the Save Nabisco Action Coalition (SNAC), comprised of labor, religious and community people. SNAC learned from a Nabisco management employee (who knew he would also lose his job if the plant closed) that the plant was profitable—earning $2 million dollars a month. SNAC also found that a member of Nabisco's board of directors was on the board of a local Pittsburgh bank, Equibank. This interlock between Nabisco and Equibank became the cornerstone of SNAC's fightback campaign.

SNAC distributed thousands of post cards, addressed to the Equibank board member, stating that each signer pledged to remove a specific amount of funds from the bank unless the decision to close Nabisco was reversed. The union also brought direct pressure. At a well-publicized rally to kick off the pledge card campaign, a representative of the union's International announced that a nationwide strike of all Nabisco plants would occur if the Pittsburgh plant was shut down. Within a few weeks, Equibank's board member received thousands of pledge cards and Nabisco decided to keep the plant open.

After their victory, SNAC did not stop fighting. Changing its name to the Support our Neighborhoods Action Coalition, it continued to build for a broader Pittsburgh movement against plant closures. SNAC worked with others to draft a local plant closures ordinance and staged its own public hearing, inviting the Pittsburgh City Council to attend. The City Council then held another hearing, passed a plant closures ordinance and overrode a veto by the Mayor. The community-drafted law would have required advance notice and the establishment of a city bureau to investigate the reason for all shutdowns and identify economic alternatives.[2] But the ordinance was overturned in Pennsylvania State Court on a technicality involving Pittsburgh's City Charter.

New Bedford Saves Morse Tool

Morse Cutting Tool is one of New Bedford, Massachusetts' oldest and largest employers. In 1982, Morse Tool's owner, the Gulf & Western Corporation, demanded large concessions from workers and threatened to close the plant. In response, the Morse workers' union, UE Local 277, arranged for the Industrial Cooperative Association (ICA) to conduct a study of G&W's management of the plant. The ICA study found that G&W appeared to be following a conscious policy of disinvestment. Concessions then, said Local 277 President Rod Poineau, "would just be financing Gulf & Western's move."

The union publicized the results of the ICA study, along with the union's modest wage and benefit proposals, at an April 1982 luncheon meeting attended by over 100 political, labor and religious leaders. When G&W turned down the union proposal, workers launched a strike that was to last 13 weeks, and the new Citizens Committee to Support the

UE

Morse Tool Workers carried out a community campaign. A petition drive called on G&W to reinvest and modernize Morse Tool or sell the plant to someone who would. The City Council passed a resolution committing the City to do everything possible to keep Morse Tool operating; the Massachusetts House of Representatives approved a similar resolution. Feeling the pressure, in early August, G&W reached a contract settlement with the union, without concessions.

Less than two years later, in April 1984, G&W announced it would either sell Morse Tool by July 31 or liquidate the company's assets and close it down. The UE analyzed the proposals made by prospective buyers and decided that none offered a secure commitment to keep the plant operating. Once again, the City of New Bedford responded. After examining legal precedent, Mayor Brian Lawler announced the City's intention to use its powers of eminent domain to take over the plant and run it, unless a suitable buyer could be found. G&W was persuaded to cancel its July 31 deadline and a new owner came forward who was acceptable to G&W, the City and the union.

Asked what advice he would give to others in the same position as Morse Tool workers, Local 277 President Ron Poineau said, "Do everything possible. Rally the city or the town behind the workers. Without the support of the community forget it! Together, we saved Morse for the City as well as for the workers."[3]

Chicago's Early Warning Network

In January 1984, the City of Chicago made a joint award of $20,000 to the Midwest Center for Labor and Research and the University of Illinois Center for Urban Economic Development to build a strong early warning network of unions, community organizations, local residents and business groups. Dan Swinney, executive director of the Midwest Center for Research, lost his job in a steel plant in 1983. The project has targeted an area of Chicago's West Side, known as the Lake Street industrial corridor, where over 45 plant closures occurred in 1982. The purpose of the network is to anticipate plant closures and mass layoffs and propose creative alternatives, employing a range of methods from recommending new product lines to providing assistance with capital investment. If successful, the project will serve as a model for other areas of the city.

Campaign for a Steel Valley Authority

Between the fall of 1977 and December of 1979, the community of Youngstown, Ohio was rocked by successive announcements of closures at three steel mills. Eventually, 10,000 jobs would be lost. At the time the first closure was announced, concerned religious leaders banded together to form the Ecumenical Coalition of the Mahoning Valley. The coalition joined with local Steelworkers Union officials and the National Center for Economic Alternatives to develop a plan for reopening the first abandoned mill under the ownership of a worker-community corporation, to be called Community Steel.

With news of each closure, local support for the concept of Community Steel increased. Worker-community ownership became the rallying point for increasingly militant activity by local steelworkers. The plan for Community Steel was expanded to encompass the other closed facilities. To demonstrate the willingness of the local community to support the venture financially, the Ecumenical Coalition launched the Save Our Valley (SOV) campaign—this community-labor-religious campaign would become an inspiration to activists around the country. Congregations and individuals were urged to open SOV accounts at area banks, earmarking the money for use as capital for Community Steel. By November 1978, over $4 million had been deposited in 4,138 SOV accounts by local residents and national religious denominations.

Yet even with such strong support, the Community Steel plan failed. Coalition members counted on the Federal Government to subsidize the estimated $400 million needed to initiate the program at the first mill. Government-financed feasibility studies were encouraging. Informal commitments were made by Carter Administration officials, but they were never honored. The Carter Administration denied the loans.

The failure of Youngstown's experiment did not mean an end to the concept of worker-community control in the steel industry. In 1979, veterans of the Ecumenical Coalition helped found the Tri-State Conference on Steel. This broader group included steelworkers and other trade unionists, unemployed workers and community activists from Ohio and Pennsylvania. While Tri-State concerns itself with the large steel-producing region of western Pennsylvania, eastern Ohio and northern West Virginia, Pennsylvania's Monongahela River Valley (Mon Valley) has become the main focus of attention.

Tri-State members pressed the idea of worker-community control in the midst of heated battles to stop the closures of steel mills, supplier plants and other industries in the Mon Valley area. Along with the Mon Valley Unemployed Committee and other groups of unemployed workers and supporters, Tri-State also helped organize food banks and fought to extend unemployment compensation benefits, provide medical care, and stop home foreclosures. Faced with the refusal of corporations to sell plants to private or community-owned enterprises which would then "compete" with them, Tri-State pushed the idea of using eminent domain to acquire abandoned mills and plants. In Pennsylvania and many other states, municipal governments have the authority to condemn, purchase and hold private property if it is deemed vital to the economic future of the community. Tri-State argued that eminent domain could be used to assist publicly planned and supported development in the same way that it has been used to aid private corporations (such as GM's Poletown plant).

In October 1983, Tri-State sponsored a conference on the revitalization of Pittsburgh's steel industry, bringing together prominent economists and industrial experts with union leaders, community activists and unemployed workers. The day long event became a model of grassroots economic development planning. The conference produced a plan calling for the establishment of a Steel Valley Authority through the action of local municipal governments. The Steel Valley Authority would be empowered to use eminent domain to acquire steel producing facilities in the Mon Valley, and sell them to private companies or worker-owners dedicated to rebuilding steel production in the area. While funded by the Federal Government, the Steel Valley Authority would be made up of local labor and community representatives.[4]

At this writing, eight municipal governments are taking steps toward formation of the Steel Valley Authority. Meanwhile, a critical struggle is underway to save U.S. Steel's highly productive "Dorothy Six" blast furnace in Duquesne, Pennsylvania. U.S. Steel wants to destroy Dorothy Six and use the land to build an industrial park. Tri-State, the United Steel Workers of America and local officials, including the Allegheny County commissioners, are trying to save the modern furnace to serve as the centerpiece of revitalized steel production in the area. The original December 1984 deadline for Dorothy's destruction was postponed under community pressure (Tri-State organized an emergency response network threatening civil disobedience if demolition equipment came into Duquesne) and hope remains that Dorothy Six will become the first victory in the campaign for community control of steel.[5]

Worker Ownership

Boycott and Buyout at Sierra Designs

In October 1984 garment workers employed by the Sierra Designs Company in Oakland, California were informed of the company's plan to close the manufacturing facility, employing about 75 people, and contract out the sewing for their line of tents, backpacks and other outdoor gear. Workers had seen the signs of a closure for months, as boxes of garments began arriving at the company warehouse from sewing shops in Hong Kong, Taiwan and Mexico. Many Oakland employees had firsthand knowledge of the horrendous working conditions

Gil Trevino-Ortiz

in those countries. About 50 percent of Sierra Designs seamstresses were Chinese immigrants, many of whom had first started sewing in Hong Kong sweatshops. Another group of workers had come from the Mexican border state of Durango.

Although previous attempts to unionize had been unsuccessful in uniting the multi-racial workforce, the mainly middle-aged women workers committed to organize themselves and others to fight the closure. They approached the Oakland-based Plant Closures Project for assistance. Initially, employee representatives and community delegations attempted to meet with Sierra Designs management to explore possible alternatives. But the company refused to meet and hired a union-busting law firm.

In early November, with the help of the Project, workers formed a community coalition which quickly decided to launch a boycott of Sierra Designs products to force the company to the bargaining table. Coalition members picketed the four retail outlets in the San Francisco Bay area and conducted a national pledge card campaign. Pledge cards stating that the signer refused to purchase any Sierra Designs products until the dispute was settled were distributed through national plant closures, labor and religious networks. Supporters were asked to mail the cards to the president of Sierra Designs and the chairman of CML Inc., the Boston-based parent company. Workers later learned that both men were swamped with cards from around the country.

The Bay area boycott was also highly effective. Sierra Designs employees worked the week sewing and on weekends joined their community supporters on lively picket lines at the stores, asking holiday shoppers to look elsewhere for gifts. Coalition members felt close to success as one retail store manager reported that the boycott had cost Sierra Designs 50 percent of its crucial Christmas sales.

The coalition also threatened to take their issue before CML's first public shareholders meeting being held in December in Boston. Armed with shareholder proxies, they promised to attend the meeting accompanied by labor and religious supporters from the Boston area unless the dispute was resolved by the evening before the shareholders meeting. A partial agreement was reached by midnight, with remaining issues settled a few days later.

Sierra Designs agreed to pay increased severance pay and extended health benefits, and it agreed to assist the workers in setting up a worker cooperative sewing shop which would contract for much of the company's production. More specifically, Sierra Designs agreed to (1) fund a feasability study to examine the viability of a coop; (2) contract a substantial amount of work to the new coop for at least three years; (3) donate equipment or sell it at reduced cost to the coop; and (4) give over 10 percent of the proceeds from the annual January sale to the workers, to be used either as start-up capital, or to be distributed as increased severance.

On April 1, 1985, the Rainbow Workers Coop, made up of 33 former Sierra Designs employees, opened for business. Workers will initially make about the same as their old wages, and prospects look good for the future. Coop board member Betty Chisolm remarks, "When the company first announced the closure, we were mad, but we thought we were helpless to do anything about it...Now I feel like we can do anything."[6]

From A&P to O&O

In February 1982, the A&P Company (previously acquired by Tenglemann, a West German corporation) gave its workers 20 days notice that it would shut down thirty of its stores in the Philadelphia area. "The bomb hit real fast," recalls Marge Bonacci, a deli manager who had worked at A&P for 25 years. "I said 'Who's going to want me? I'm almost 60 years old.'"[7] But with the help of her union, Local 1357 of the United Food and Commercial Workers (UFCW), and the Philadelphia Association for Cooperative Ownership (PACE), workers in Bonacci's Roslyn store and another in Parkwood Manor took over two of the A&P stores themselves. They are now successful worker cooperatives called "O&O" or Employee Owned and Operated Supermarkets.

Local 1357 and PACE put together an initial plan to buy out 21 of the stores. After two months of negotiations, A&P agreed to continue operating stores under its new subsidiary, Super Fresh, in return for union concessions, including a 20 percent pay cut and reduced vacation and overtime premium pay. A&P also agreed to facilitate future worker buyouts and startups of worker-owned enterprises by contributing 1 percent of gross annual sales to a union-controlled trust, with the bulk of the money to go to workers as yearly wage bonuses and the remainder to capitalize an employee ownership investment fund.

PACE carried out an extensive education and training program on how to run cooperative enterprises. While most of the former A&P workers were rehired by Super Fresh, 50 opted to become worker-owners

assisted by loans from the Local's Federal Credit Union and bank financing backed by loan guarantees from the federal Small Business Administration.

Marge Bonacci describes her initial misgivings about the workers running their own store: "When it first started out, I thought, 'Oh, my God, we'll never be able to do this. We're not smart enough!' I was a deli person. I sliced lunchmeat. How do I know what a manager does?"[8] As described in *Changing Work*, the two O&O's are "democratically-managed by worker-owner committees that set store policies, hire and fire managers, and share profits among member workers on the basis of hours worked." The Roslyn O&O outsells the former A&P by 40 percent and Parkwood Manor outsells it by 20 percent. "Because they do not have to support a corporate superstructure with high-priced executives...the O&O's have lowered overhead costs, and can attract customers with prices consistently below those of their competitors."[9]

"You spend 19 years figuring out what you would do if it was your place," says Leo Maiorini, cooperative president, "but you don't have that freedom to explore. It's something you dream about."[10] Now the workers can explore what's best for their customers and themselves. They expanded the ethnic food section and added bulk ice cream. Bonacci, now the cooperative secretary and deli manager, picks and chooses among vendors and sells her own meatballs at the deli counter.

A third O&O will open in 1985 in North Philadelphia, as part of a city-backed economic development project. PACE is also working with Spring Garden United Neighbors, mostly low and moderate income Black and Latino residents, to plan for a fourth O&O. In the words of PACE lawyer Andy Lamas, "The O&O experience demonstrates the enormous potential for building meaningful alliances between the cooperative movement and the labor movement."[11]

Economic Conversion

Increasingly workers have begun to realize that plants, equipment and their own skills can be recycled to produce new products in plants that might otherwise be shut down for economic or social reasons by transferring resources from unnecessary weapons systems to human services, for example. The inspiration for conversion to production of alternative products, or "Alternative Use," came from British workers at Lucas Aerospace.

Lucas Aerospace: Alternatives to Military Production

Lucas Aerospace is Britain's largest military contractor and like similar U.S. firms, Lucas introduced automated technology into its plants; between 1970 and 1976 employment at Lucas was reduced from

17,000 to 12,000. Anticipating further job loss, shop stewards from each Lucas Aerospace plant elected delegates to a Combine Shop Steward Committee to coordinate a worker response to company policy on a company-wide basis. Shop stewards went back to their plants and asked Lucas workers to inventory equipment and technical skills on site and suggest new products which could be produced with those resources. In April 1976, the Combine Shop Steward Committee publicly released a 1,200 page Alternative Corporate Plan which included 200 non-military products in various areas, including transportation, energy and medical equipment. The objective of the plan was to use technology to upgrade workers' skills and to produce socially useful products.

Lucas Aerospace management rejected the plan, claiming that the best way to protect the jobs of Lucas workers would be to continue concentrating on military production. When 2,000 Liverpool workers were laid off by Lucas in 1978, the workers took their problem to the government. In 1979, a compromise was reached between the government, Lucas management and the shop stewards to try some aspects of the Alternative Corporate Plan in Lucas factories in Liverpool. Later, the Greater London Council funded a municipal council on conversion alternatives for the city.

U.S. Initiatives

The Center for Economic Conversion is building on the Lucas experience by providing an economic conversion clearinghouse and organizing assistance to conversion efforts in the U.S. and Canada. Formerly known as the Mid-Peninsula Conversion Project, the Center was originally established as an effort by community, religious and labor activists in California's Santa Clara Valley to promote the conversion of plants to non-military uses.

There is a growing list of conversion projects. In the Atomic Reclamation and Conversion Project in Piketon, Ohio, the Oil, Chemical, and Atomic Workers Union (OCAW) is developing alternative plans for three military nuclear reprocessing plants. Under the Franklin County Development Corporation worker councils are being organized in western Massachusetts to identify alternative products for the troubled cutting tool industry. The International Association of Machinists & Aerospace Workers (IAM) is organizing for conversion by developing an educational curriculum to improve rank and file engineering skills and by conducting surveys of their members for conversion ideas. UE members who work in a GE plant in Charleston, South Carolina, producing nuclear and non-nuclear generator equipment and scheduled to close down, are setting up worker councils to look into alternative products. The worker councils were organized with the help of the Greater London Conversion Council as a direct result of a workshop held at a 1984 International Conversion Conference discussed later.

Two bills have been introduced into the House of Representatives supporting economic conversion from military production. The Defense

Economic Adjustment Act (HR 425), introduced by Representative Ted Weiss of New York, would make the federal government responsible for supporting economic conversion planning in the defense sector, with provisions for a Defense Economic Adjustment Council, Community Economic Adjustment Planning, Alternative Use Committees in the plants, and Economic Adjustment Assistance for Workers. The Economic Conversion Act (HR 4805) would, in the words of its sponsor, Representative Nicholas Mavroules of Massachusetts, "sound an economic declaration of independence for communities uncomfortably tied to defense dollars." It would provide for advance notification of cutbacks in military spending, alternative production and job retraining planning grants, and temporary income for unemployed defense workers.

Plant Closure Legislation

When Scoa Industries went out of the shoemaking business in 1981, it paid about $1.8 million in severance to 800 employees at the two Maine factories of its Norrwock Shoe Company, and donated the plants to the two towns so that they could find suitable operators. The severance pay was distributed under a Maine law requiring 60 days notice of plant closures and severance pay based on one week's pay for each year of employment for all who have worked in the plant for at least three years.[12] Maine is one of two states which have already enacted plant closure legislation; Wisconsin is the other. Legislation has been introduced in about twenty state legislatures. As in the California case below, these bills often result from grassroots organizing efforts.

Grassroots Action for Legislation in California

When California became number three on the list of states hit hardest by plant closures, Californians Against Plant Shutdowns (CAL-CAPS) was organized as a statewide network of community-labor coalitions working together for protective legislation. In June 1982, labor, community and religious activists mobilized around the state and packed a California State Assembly Ways and Means Committee hearing on a plant closures bill introduced by Assembly member Maxine Waters. The continuing effort to pass state legislation has not been successful, but plant closures legislation has been enacted in Vacaville and is being considered in other communities around California.

The Vacaville ordinance is particularly important because it is presently the strongest plant closures law in the country and it is also a model for tempering some of the incentives that cities use to attract runaway shops from neighboring areas. In January 1983, Simpson Dura-Vent, a stove pipe manufacturer in Redwood City, California, announced plans to relocate to Vacaville, taking advantage of $2.5 million in low-interest loans being offered by the Vacaville Redevelopment Agency as an incentive to attract business to its 3,300 acre industrial park. The United Electrical Workers Union proposed several alternatives to the company in an effort to save the jobs of its Redwood City members, 90 percent of whom were Latino. The union identified an alternative site for plant relocation in nearby Union City and, when the company rejected that site, the union insisted that Redwood City workers be transferred to Vacaville with the plant. When Simpson Dura-Vent replied that it was under no obligation to transfer any employees, the union joined forces with the Oakland Plant Closures Project to fight a classic runaway shop situation: Simpson Dura-Vent planned to bust the union and pay its Vacaville workers 33 percent less than its union rates in Redwood City.

In order to pressure Vacaville officials to aid them in getting Simpson Dura-Vent to the bargaining table, attorneys for UE and the Plant Closures Project filed suit against the city's redevelopment plan on the grounds of two technical violations of State redevelopment law: (1) Vacaville had sidestepped a law which forbids one city to "raid" the industry of another, by calling itself a "redevelopment agency" instead of a city and (2) while State law requires that redevelopment areas are "blighted," Vacaville was actually converting thousands of acres of prime agricultural land to prime industrial land. The two sides arrived at an agreement which preserved the redevelopment plan while establishing guidelines for companies that move to Vacaville and receive publicly subsidized financing: such firms must comply with affirmative action guidelines, recognize the union representing workers at the company's old site and provide at least one year's notice of shutdowns or layoffs.

Simpson Dura-Vent refused to meet the conditions of this agreement and lost its financing deal with the city. In retaliation, the company filed suit against UE International and the Local, the Plant Closures Project

and the City of Vacaville. Part of the lawsuit asked for a ruling against
the agreement on the grounds that local governments' jurisdiction to
legislate in plant closure situations is preempted by national labor law;
this argument was used unsuccessfully in the court case against
Pittsburgh's plant closure ordinance. Other land developers also filed
suit about issues in the agreement, and the ruling was revised 15 times
before it finally passed as a city ordinance in January 1984, at which time
the developers dropped their suit. Soon after, Simpson Dura-Vent agreed
to drop its lawsuit and signed a last-minute severance agreement with the
UE.

The Vacaville ordinance requires any employer who wants to
receive low-interest loans or other financial assistance from Vacaville's
Redevelopment Agency to: give mandatory three months advance notice
to employees who will be laid off if the company is shutting down,
moving or reducing operations; make every reasonable effort to provide
one year or more advance notice; present the City with an affirmative
action plan for the hiring, training and upgrading of minority workers;
provide its union with notice of its application for low-interest loans or
other financial assistance if it is relocating to Vacaville from another
California City.

National Legislation

In order to curtail the senseless competition between states and cities
for jobs and investment, a longterm goal of the plant closure movement
is to enact comprehensive federal legislation. Several national bills have
already been introduced in Congress. The most recent version is HR
2847, introduced in 1983 by Congressman Ford of Michigan. The bill
calls for up to a year's advance notice of a closure, retraining, severance
benefits, and corporate reimbursement to affected communities, including 300 percent of tax revenues lost due to a company moving overseas.
The bill would also provide assistance to business concerns threatened
with closure and to worker associations that are trying to buy out a
company.

Mike Peters

Developing International Solidarity

There is strong agreement within the plant closures movement that the best way to counter runaway shops and exploitation by multinational corporations is to achieve international solidarity for the rights of *all* workers in the U.S. and overseas. The following examples are positive steps in forging a global response to plant closures through grassroots connections and proposed legislation.

Plant Closures Project International Connections Task Force

The International Connections Task Force of the Plant Closures Project in Oakland holds forums with visiting organizers from other countries and does solidarity work, such as obtaining letters of foreign support for the GE workers in Ontario. In 1984, the Task Force sent six American workers on tour to meet with workers in Japan, South Korea and Taiwan. The trip provided a first-hand opportunity to break through misconceptions on both sides. "It was important to let people know that conditions in the U.S. aren't as sweet as everyone thinks they are," says Joe Regacho of the Plant Closures Project. "What we have in common is that we're all being taken advantage of. We saw real concretely, global competition for lower wages and how that works. It was easy to see how businesses are playing countries against each other. You saw that when the Philippines lowered its wages, Hong Kong lowered its wages even further to attract business." Looking to the future, Regacho says, "We want to build up our International Connections Task Force to start the groundwork for organizing on a global basis. Realistically, that's the only way we can look at the world."[13]

U.S.-Mexico Border Network

In 1981, workers from Mexico participated in the First Western International Conference on Economic Dislocation held in Los Angeles, and formed lasting connections with activists in the Los Angeles Coalition Against Shutdowns. Building on those contacts, in 1984, LACAPS joined with the Centro de Estudios Fronterisos of Tijuana, Mexico, the Tucson Metropolitan Ministry, the American Friends Service Committee, and worker organizations on both sides of the border to organize a cross-border network and bilingual newsletter called *Boletin Informativo Puente* or *Bridge Over the Border*. "The purpose of the network," says Kathy Seal of LACAPS, "will be to create cross-border solidarity which may be translated into action in the future."[14]

Project organizers agree that the best strategy to counter the attraction of U.S. corporate runaways to Mexico is to help Mexican workers in their struggle for better wages and living standards. A primary focus of the Network is to provide support for employees of *maquiladoras*, assembly plants of U.S. companies with operations on both sides of the border. There are over 600 *maquiladoras*, assembling such items as pre-cut garments and electronic components. Most of the workers are young women, 16 to 25 years of age, averaging 48 hours a week on the job at Mexican minimum wage (equivalent to about 77 cents an hour in 1983); companies routinely violate even this low minimum wage.[15] The Network initiated action by organizing support for striking Zenith workers in Reynosa, Mexico.

International Economic Conversion Conference

The first International Economic Conversion Conference (IECC) was held in Boston in June 1984. More than 700 people attended, from 41 states and 13 countries; 49 different unions were represented, including 19 from other countries. Conference discussions related conversion to issues of peace, economic security and social justice, and "nuts and bolts" workshops were held in eight industry areas to help workers plan for conversion. The conference provided an important meeting ground for peace and labor activists to come together. "For the first time," said a representative of the Oil, Chemical and Atomic Workers Union, "I saw people who've been holding vigils outside defense contractors' gates meeting with workers from inside the same factories. The peaceniks weren't telling workers how bad they are because they build weapons. They were asking how they could help them. And the workers weren't attacking the peaceniks because they're 'anti-jobs.' I think what we're seeing here is the creation of a new and growing labor-peace alliance."

The conference heard moving presentations from labor leaders in other countries, including Chris Dlamini, president of the Federation of South African Trade Unions (FOSATU) and an employee of the Kellogg Cereal plant in Johannesburg. Dlamini was arrested in November 1984, when FOSATU joined a two day mass strike to protest apartheid in concert with student and community groups under the umbrella of the United Democratic Front. The IECC helped organize an international campaign to free Dlamini and other labor leaders arrested under a security law providing for indefinite detention without charges in solitary confinement.

TIE: Transnationals Information Exchange

TIE was established in 1978 in response to a growing awareness that nationally-based union organizing is no longer adequate to meet the challenge of a world economy dominated by multinational corporations. Based in Europe, and comprised of about 40 action/research groups and workers' organizations, TIE has established committees to promote the exchange of information and experience between workers in the auto industry, new technology and agribusiness.

In 1982, one member organization of the TIE network brought together 60 employees of the Philips corporation from all over Europe, Columbia, Brazil and India. TIE has also worked to establish or strengthen international connections between workers around the world who are employed by Peugeot-Citroen-Talbot, Ford, and Massey-Ferguson. The *TIE Report* broadens the outreach function of the network by publishing reports on TIE activities, company profiles and in-depth articles on specific companies and industries.

International Sugar Workers Cooperative

Building on a historical network which existed between northern and southern U.S. refinery workers, an effort was begun in the late 1970s to establish connections among the Sugar Workers of Amstar, a major multinational sugar company, as well as between other U.S. and foreign companies. In 1983, a network called the International Sugar Workers Cooperative was formed with a Western Region, including workers in North America, Hawaii and the Philippines, and a newsletter called *Sugar World* or *Mundo Azucarero*, funded by the Canadian Council of Churches. Through the efforts of *Sugar World*, the International Commission for the Coordination of Solidarity Among Sugar Workers was founded at a 1983 conference in Toronto, Canada, attended by sugar workers from 20 countries and conducted in four languages.

According to Ken Dursa of Sugar Workers Local 180 in Salinas, California, this network allows workers "to organize on the same level and extent as the companies and get a real sophisticated view of how the industry actually works. The more we understand how the industry works, the more we will be able to work on a practical basis to change it. And, by organizing all of the workers of one company on an international basis, we can see that our problem is the company—not people from different countries."[16]

International Legislation and Policy

The Vredling Directive

In recent years, the European Economic Community (EEC), an association of ten European nations known as the Common Market, has considered passage of the "Vredling Directive." It would establish the first legally binding disclosure legislation to cover multinational corporations and require corporations in Europe to provide trade union representatives with advance notice of plant closures and plans to relocate or merge with another company.

The Vredling Directive has been attacked by a very aggressive American business lobby. The Directive would affect all U.S. firms with foreign subsidiaries in Europe. And if European employees of U.S. owned corporations have access to information about corporate finances, plans and policies, it will make it much easier for American workers to obtain the same information. The Vredling proposal has wide support from the 10 Common Market nations and even if the unanimous vote that is needed to pass the Directive is not attained, it is very likely that some of the countries will eventually adopt the law on their own.

Linking Trade Policy and Workers Rights

In the summer of 1983, the Washington-based Interfaith Action for Economic Justice met with a broad group of human rights organizations, unions and policy analysts to explore how trade policy was encouraging runaway shops and what could be done to change it. The group decided upon a legislative strategy to link one policy, the "Graduated System of Preferences," to plant closures in the U.S. and worker rights overseas. The Graduated System of Preferences (GSP) was established in the 1960s, when the world's largest industrialized nations agreed to provide unilateral trade benefits to 114 countries and territories. Many of these countries have repressive governments which deny workers basic rights.

The Interfaith Action group proposed conditions for renewal of the GSP, requiring that beneficiaries respect "internationally recognized rights of workers," such as the right to organize, and a bill stipulating these conditions was introduced in the House of Representatives by Congressman Donald Pease of Ohio. In October 1984, Congress passed legislation renewing the GSP which contained the Pease Amendment. Before this victory, International Action for Economic Justice staff member Carole Collins had explained, "By eliminating GSP benefits to repressive governments, we eliminate the downward pressure on U.S. wages and working conditions which occurs when American-based multinational corporations run away to low-wage countries. By supporting the labor rights of workers in the Third World, we can help stop plant closures in the U.S."[17]

CREATING A JUST ECONOMY

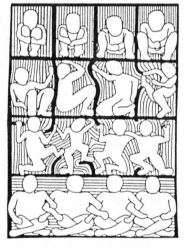

As more and more workers and communities have joined together to fight plant closures, they have stopped blaming themselves, each other and foreign workers, and started blaming an economic system which values only the needs of capital. Contrary to the old saying, "What's Good for GM is Good for the Country," capital and working people have very different needs.

Capital seeks absolute mobility, to move anywhere, anytime, in search of cheaper, regimented labor and larger government handouts. But people require job and income security to support themselves and their families and develop strong communities. Capital needs to control the labor process, and continually deskills and dehumanizes work to meet narrowly-defined criteria of economic efficiency.

On the community level, these opposing needs lead to conflicting interpretations of economic reality, such as what is a cost and what is a benefit. For example, the company considers its payroll a cost—the lower the better. But to the community, higher paychecks are clearly a benefit. Rising profit earned by the company is an obvious benefit in the eyes of owners, managers and shareholders. But, as long as the profit is reinvested outside of the community, it will rate as a zero on the community's ledger. And when the company shuts down its local operations, the community registers costs which will never appear in the company's books.

The growing wave of plant closures has fostered a rising sense of outrage over the dominance of capital's needs over people's needs. In the words of William Winpisinger, president of the International Association of Machinists and Aerospace Workers (IAM):

By what holy writ does capital...have the right to meet as small groups in the boardroom and recast the lifestyles and livelihoods of American workers? ...Everything else has democratic controls on it, including labor...but there are none on capital.[1]

A 1982 Pastoral Letter by the Episcopal Urban Bishops Coalition warned, "We know of no more sinister power and threat to the welfare of the human community than that flowing from corporate structures which remove control of resources and decision-making from the people most affected."

To take control of our future we must gain more control over today's economic decisions. We must be able to plan ahead, not just clean up in the wake of corporate irresponsibility. We need a national program which attacks the *causes* of plant closures—unchecked capital mobility, wasteful mergers, unfair tax policies, military waste of public resources, misguided foreign policy—and not only the symptoms of unemployment and economic dislocation.

Voices for Change

There have already been significant efforts by progressive political, religious and labor leaders to translate the values of a just economy into comprehensive proposals for national policy. For example, the 1981 *Alternative Budget Resolution of the Congressional Black Caucus* sets forth a comprehensive national budget designed, in part, to challenge attacks on federally-funded social programs and "To help achieve a full employment economy aimed at improving the quality of life for all Americans, particularly the poor, working and middle income."

Also in 1981, the International Association of Machinists and Aerospace Workers presented a detailed *Rebuilding America Act*, including a Technology Bill of Rights. The program would require corporations to operate under a federal charter and protect the rights of workers to organize, safeguard workplace and environmental health and safety, and contribute to a Federal Investment Reserve Fund. It would establish a Federal Investment and Production Office which would promote full employment, economic growth and price stability. It would also create a Federal Pension Fund Bank to invest pension funds in the best interest of workers and a National Employment Opportunity Service to link workers with jobs around the country. Under the *Rebuilding America Act*, cities would be reconstructed through a federally-financed and community-controlled program. The tax system would be overhauled to eliminate corporate loopholes and reduce the burden on poor and middle income Americans. A Technology Bill of Rights would ensure that technology be used to strengthen the economy and benefit workers and communities.[2]

In November 1984, the National Conference of Catholic Bishops presented the first draft of their *Pastoral Letter on Catholic Social Teaching and the U.S. Economy*. Four years in the making, the Letter is considered one of the most significant in the history of the American church. It is guided by "Three priority principles": "Fulfillment of the basic needs of the poor is of highest priority; increased participation in society by people living on its margins takes priority over the preservation of privileged concentrations of power, wealth, and income; and meeting human needs and increasing participation should be priority targets in the investment of wealth, talent, and human energy.''[3]

Linking the need for a just U.S. economy with the need for a humane foreign policy, the *Pastoral Letter* suggests some standards for national policy, including:

1. The federal government should create an active program to reduce unemployment and create jobs.
2. Resources should be diverted away from the arms race—which hurts the economy—and channeled into creating a more just and productive economy.
3. Labor laws should be reformed so that they encourage rather than inhibit the development of unions.
4. U.S. foreign policy should be redirected away from military programs and concentrate on basic human needs.

By asserting economic values which serve human needs and aspirations, the above proposals help illuminate an alternative vision for the future: a future where everyone can contribute to and benefit from building a strong and just economy; where tax dollars are spent to improve public services, working conditions and living standards; and where foreign workers can organize for better wages and working conditions, without fear of U.S. intervention—until there is no place left where corporations can run to.

This vision will not become a reality unless we build a broad constituency to support it. The experience of the plant closures movement provides some crucial lessons for the task ahead.

Building A Grassroots Movement for a Just Economy

The plant closures movement is only one of many grassroots efforts in the United States which share a longterm goal of building a just economy. Born of diverse experiences, these contemporary movements have in common the practice of exposing myths and challenging corporate economic values; building bridges between constituencies who have not worked together in the past; and encouraging people to "think globally, and act locally."

The greatest power of these movements lies in their potential to join forces, by linking issues in organizing and educational campaigns and creating strong working relationships between organizations. In this way, the creation of community-labor coalitions was a watershed development in the fight against plant closures. The most significant

I'M SORRY WE HAVE TO FORECLOSE ON YOUR FARM, BUT AGRICULTURE IS IN TRANSITION...

AND THE FAMILY FARM IS THE VICTIM OF CHANGING ECONOMIC REALITIES

result of unity among diverse constituencies has been to gradually shift attention from narrow fights to save particular jobs to the question of how to provide for the economic health of the community as a whole.

We can include here the growing efforts of community, labor, health and environmental organizations which combat the problem of toxics in the community and workplace. They assert that poisons are not a necessary cost of progress and that workers do not have to choose between their jobs and their health. In Silicon Valley, California, many electronics plants have shut down with little or no advance notice, leaving startled communities with poisoned wells and other environmental problems, as well as economic hardship. The Plant Closures Project and the Silicon Valley Toxics Coalition have joined forces to fight for advance notice of shutdowns and, thus, improve their ability to respond to environmental and economic threats to the community. Today the Plant Closures Project has a seat on the Toxics Coalition governing board.[4]

The Jobs with Peace campaign is another example of effective coalition building and grassroots organizing. Mobilizing a united front among labor and peace activists, the campaign has passed Jobs with Peace referenda in over 70 cities across the country, educating communities about the harmful impact of military spending on the economy and demanding alternative local and federal spending priorities.

We can also see progress in the growing unity among industrial workers producing farm equipment and Midwestern farmers fighting foreclosures. In early 1985, United Auto Workers President Owen Bieber spoke to the National Farmers Union Convention in Phoenix. He pledged industrial workers' support of farmers' demands for credit relief, stating that both groups are fighting "a vicious, dishonest mentality that says farms must be foreclosed and factories must be boarded up because 'market forces' dictate those outcomes." He pledged that UAW members "will be with you and stay with you until the politicians understand that they must either move with the agenda of rural America or get out of the way, because we are moving with the unstoppable power of collective action."[5]

A key strategy in transforming the economy is to create positive economic alternatives wherever and whenever possible. The worker/community initiatives which appear throughout this booklet provide

BUT SOCIETY DOES OWE YOU PEOPLE SOMETHING, AND WE'LL TAKE CARE OF YOU—

JUST LIKE WE DID THE STEELWORKERS

Wasserman

Military Spending vs. Human Needs

Military Program	Cost	Alternatives
1 A-6E Intruder Aircraft	$9 million	100,000 youths employed at minimum wage for 1 year
1 F-14 Jet Fighter	$15.6 million	500 low-cost, 2 bedroom homes
1 C-5A Cargo Plane	$60 million	food for 12,000 families of 4 for 1 year
2 B-1 Bombers	$400 million	cost of rebuilding Cleveland's water supply system
Cruise Missile Program	$11 billion	cost of bringing annual rate of investment in public works to 1965 levels

Source: Dick Gillett, "...But What Are We For? A Proposal to Stimulate Discussion Within the Christian Community about Alternative Public Policies and Goals," Unpublished Paper, 1984.

glimpses of a more just economic future. The Vacaville Ordinance tempers regional competition and requires corporations to meet obligations to workers and communities before taking advantage of government subsidies. The Philadelphia O&O workers showed they could take over their stores and run them as successful, democratic, community-oriented enterprises. The Tri-State proposal for a Steel Valley Authority is a blueprint for large-scale community control.

All these initiatives are steps toward economic structures which value the needs of community over capital. Through them we can learn more about how a just economic system can work, and how we can organize to achieve it. By linking issues, organizations and movements, we can expand our capabilities and vision, and move closer to gaining a broad popular consensus around the values of a just economy and society.

From "Grand Performance" Mural, Oakland, CA
Keith Sklar and Daniel Galvez

FOOTNOTES

Chapter 1
1. "GE Employee Communicator," December 11, 1979; "The Fight to Save the Ontario GE Iron Plant," UE Local 1012, 1981.
2. Richard Gillett, "Case Study: California General Electric Iron Factory Sacrificed to Singapore," *The Witness*, September 1982.
3. *Los Angeles Times*, July 27, 1981.
4. *Los Angeles Times*, July 26, 1981.
5. Interview with Mary McDaniel by Gilda Haas, July 30, 1984. All comments by McDaniel from this interview unless noted otherwise.
6. *Los Angeles Times*, July 27, 1981 and November 29, 1982.
7. *Los Angeles Times*, July 22, 1981.
8. "Discounters Buy Up Metal Irons," *Retailing Home Furnishings*, September 21, 1981.
9. *Los Angeles Times*, February 12, 1982.
10. Bureau of National Affairs, "Layoffs, Plant Closings, and Concession Bargaining," Washington, D.C. 1983.
11. Interview with Judi Harris by Kathy Seal, October 27, 1982. All comments by Harris from this interview unless noted otherwise.
12. Interview with Leona Setty by Joan Trafecanty, October 17, 1982.
13. Interview with E.N. Cheatham by Kathy Seal, October 27, 1982.
14. Sidney Cobb and Stanislaw Kasl, "Termination: The Consequences of Job Loss," Public Health Service, National Institute for Occupational Safety and Health, HEW, June 1977, p. 134, cited in Barry Bluestone and Bennett Harrison,*The Deindustrialization of America*, (New York: Basic Books), p. 65.
15. Harvey Brenner, "Estimating the Social Costs of National Economic Policy," Joint Economic Committee, U.S. Congress, 1976, cited in Bluestone and Harrison, *Deindustrialization*, p. 65.
16. *New York Times*, June 28, 1984.
17. *Los Angeles Times*, November 29, 1982.
18. *New York Times*, December 2, 1984.
19. *Business Week*, October 18, 1982.
20. *Wall Street Journal*, March 29, 1984; *Business Week*, January 9, 1984.
21. See William Bluestein, *Economic Notes*, February 1984; *San Francisco Chronicle*, April 22, 1983; and *Fortune*, April 30, 1984.
22. Henry Unger, "Anatomy of a Shutdown," *UE Organizer*, 1982.
23. Henry Unger, "Capping Corporate Flight," *The Progressive*, December 1982.
24. Interview with Barbara Reisman, Research Department, United Electrical Workers International, by Gilda Haas, August 6, 1984.

Chapter Two
1. *Business Week*, October 24, 1983.
2. Institute for Labor Education and Research, *What's Wrong With The U.S. Economy*, (Boston: South End Press, 1982), pp. 2, 11.
3. Harley Shaiken, *Dollars and Sense*, January 1982.
4. Ruth Leger Sivard, *World Military and Social Expenditures 1983*, (Washington, D.C.: World Priorities, 1983).
5. Ira Magaziner and Robert Reich, *Minding America's Business*, (Vintage Books, 1983), pp. 11-25.
6. Workers' Policy Project, *It's Time for Management Concessions*, 1983.
7. Robert S. McIntyre and Dean C. Tipps, *Inequity and Decline*, (Washington, D.C.: Center on Budget and Policy Priorities, 1983).
8. Center on Budget and Policy Priorities, *End Results: The Impact of Federal Policies Since 1980 On Low Income Americans*, (Washington, D.C.: Interfaith Action for Social Justice, 1984), pp. 11 and 17.
9. *San Francisco Chronicle*, April 22, 1983.

10. McIntyre and Tipps, *Inequity and Decline.*
11. *End Results*, p. 12
12. Richard Kazis and Richard L. Grossman, *Fear at Work*, (New York: Pilgrim Press, 1982).
13. *Ibid.*
14. See Charles Piller, "Job Blackmail is Industry Bluff," *In These Times*, April 6-12, 1983, and Institute for Labor Education and Research, *We Are Not The Problem!*, New York, 1982.
15. Magaziner and Reich, *Minding America's Business*, p. 165.

Chapter Three
1. Susan Holbrook, "Setting Up Production Overseas: A Primer for Management," *California Business*, April 1984.
2. Bluestone and Harrison, *Deindustrialization*, p. 42.
3. Jeremy Brecher, "Crisis Economy: Born-Again Labor Movement?"*Monthly Review*, March 1984, pp. 3-4.
4. *Ward's Auto World*, May 1983; *Automotive News*, January 31, 1983.
5. Barry Bluestone, "De-Industrializing America," transcript of speech, Western International Conference on Economic Dislocation, November 6, 1981.
6. Bluestone and Harrison, *Deindustrialization*, pp. 175-177.
7. *Ibid.*, pp. 146-147.
8. *Forbes*, March 11, 1985.
9. Bluestone and Harrison, *Deindustrialization.*
10. *Los Angeles Times*, April 29, 1984.
11. "Will Money Managers Wreck the Economy?" *Business Week*, August 13, 1984.
12. William Greider, "Taking Care of Business," *Rolling Stone*, December 9, 1982.
13. Milton Moskowitz, Michael Katz and Robert Leverling, eds., *Everybody's Business: An Almanac*, (New York: Harper & Row, 1980), p. 595.
14. California Newsreel, Transcript of film, *The Business of America*, 1984.
15. *Ibid.*
16. *Business Week*, February 25, 1985.
17. *Los Angeles Times*, January 1, 1984.
18. Bluestone and Harrison, *Deindustrialization*, p. 4.
19. *The Business of America.*
20. Midwest Center for Labor Research, *Labor Research Review*, Winter 1983.
21. Robert Goodman, *The Last Entrepreneurs: America's Regional Wars for Jobs and Dollars*, (Boston: South End Press, 1982), p. 11.
22. *Ibid.*, pp. 35-37.
23. *Ibid.*, p. 4. Bluestone and Harrison, *Deindustrialization*, p. 184.
25. Bluestone and Harrison, *Deindustrialization.*
26. Tom Barry, Beth Wood, Deb Preusch, *Dollars and Dictators*, (Albuquerque: The Resource Center, 1982).
27. *Ibid.*, p. 3.
28. *Dollars and Dictators.*
29. Joel Rocamora, "Testimonies on Economic Repression: U.S. Imperialism and the Economic Crisis of the Marcos Dictatorship," *Philippines: Repression & Resistance*, KSP, London, 1980.
30. Walden Bello, David Kinley, and Elaine Elinson, *Development Debacle: The World Bank in the Philippines*, (San Francisco: Institute for Food and Development Policy/Philippine Solidarity Network, 1982).

Chapter 4
1. Barry Bluestone, Bennett Harrison, Lucy Gorham, *Storm Clouds on the Horizon*, (Boston: Economics Education Project, May 1984).
2. *Christian Science Monitor*, September 7, 1983.
3. *Business Week*, July 9, 1984, p. 83.
4. *Occupational Outlook Handbook*, Bureau of Labor Statistics, U.S. Department of Labor, April 1984.
5. *New York Times*, May 20, 1984.

6. Richard W. Riche, Daniel E. Hecker, John U. Burgan, "High Technology Today and Tomorrow: A Small Slice of the Employment Pie," *Monthly Labor Review*, Bureau of Labor Statistics, November 1983.
7. Michael Hilliar, "High-Tech and Minority Workers," *Economic Notes*, February 1984.
8. *Christian Science Monitor*, September 12, 1983.
9. Tim Shorrock, "Atari Moves to Asia," *Multinational Monitor*, April 1983.
10. *Ibid.*
11. Philip Shapira and Jean Ross, "Closures and Layoffs in High-tech Sectors in California," Plant Closures Research Group, Department of City and Regional Planning, University of California, Berkeley, January 1984.
12. *Los Angeles Times*, June 2, 1983.
13. Claude Reed Jr., "The American Auto Industry and Black Unemployment."
14. Janet L. Norwood, Commissioner, Bureau of Labor Statistics, Testimony before the Joint Economic Committee, U.S. Congress, September 3, 1982.
15. Reed, "The American Auto Industry and Black Unemployment."
16. Interview with Elizabeth Stanley by Gilda Haas, September 1, 1984.
17. Bluestone and Harrison, *Deindustrialization*.
18. *Christian Science Monitor*, September 12, 1983.
19. Hearings before the SubCommittee on Investigations and Oversight of the Committee on Science and Technology, U.S. House of Representatives, April 6, 1983.
20. *Oakland Tribune*, April 27, 1981.
21. *Northern California Labor*, March 13, 1981.

Chapter 5
1. From California Newsreel film, *The Business of America*, 1984.
2. Interview with Rick Flanagan by Gilda Haas, May 23, 1984.
3. Dan Swinney, et. al., "Labor Community Unity," *Labor Research Review*, I:1; Martha McDevitt and Albert Van Oortmerssen, "Community Responds to Disinvestment," *TIE Report*, No.18-19; Bill Maddocks, "Morse Tool Saved by Threat of Takeover by City," *Labor Notes*, April 1985.
4. Tri-State Conference on Steel, *Steel Valley Authority: A Community Plan to Save Pittsburgh's Steel Industry*.
5. Staughton Lynd, *The Fight Against Shutdowns* (Singlejack Books, 1983); Robert Erickson, "U.S. Steelworkers Respond to Shutdowns," *TIE Report*, No. 18-19; Judy Ruszkowski and Jim Benn, "Tri-State Coalition Fights to Save the Mon Valley," *Labor Notes*, April 1985.
6. Interview with Betty Chisolm by Jan Gilbrecht, April 27, 1985.
7. *Wall Street Journal*, August 18, 1983.
8. *New York Times Magazine*, September 11, 1983.
9. Frank Lindenfeld, "O&O Markets: The Labor and Cooperative Movements Get Together," *Changing Work*, Fall 1984.
10. *Wall Street Journal*, August 18, 1983.
11. Lindenfeld, "O&O Markets."
12. *Los Angeles Times*, January 1, 1983.
13. Interview with Joe Regacho by Gilda Haas, May 23, 1984.
14. Interview with Kathy Seal by Gilda Haas, May 23, 1984.
15. Annette Fuentes and Barbara Ehrenreich, *Women in the Global Factory*, (Boston: South End Press, 1983).
16. Interview with Ken Dursa by Gilda Haas, June 1, 1984.
17. Interview with Carole Collins by Gilda Haas, June 1, 1984.

Chapter 6
1. *Barrons*, January 30, 1984.
2. International Association of Machinists and Aerospace Workers, *Let's Rebuild America*, (Washington, D.C.: Kelly Press, 1983/1984).
3. See, for example, "Community, Poverty, Justice," *Christianity and Crisis*, January 21, 1985.
4. Interview with Jan Gilbrecht by Gilda Haas, August 1, 1985.
5. *Racine Labor*, March 15, 1985.

SELECTED READINGS

Bluestone, Barry; Harrison, Bennett; and Baker, Lawrence. *Corporate Flight.* Progressive Alliance, March 1981.

Bluestone, Barry and Harrison, Bennett. *The Deindustrialization of America.* New York: Basic Books, 1982.

Citizens Labor Committee on Plant Closures. *Stop Runaway Shops.* Los Angeles, California.

Cooley, Mike. *Architect or Bee: the Human/Technology Relationship.* Chapter 4: "Drawing Up the Corporate Plan at Lucas Aerospace." Boston: South End Press, 1980.

Doherty, Barbara. *The Struggle to Save Morse Cutting Tool: A Successful Community Campaign.* North Dartmouth, MA: Labor Studies Center, Southeastern Massachusetts University, 1985.

Economic Dislocation, Plant Closing, Plant Relocation and Plant Conversion: Policies and Programs in Three Countries, Recommendations for the U.S.. A joint report of European labor union study tour participants from the UAW, USWA, and IAM, 1979.

Fuentes, Annette and Ehrenreich, Barbara. *Women in the Global Factory.* Boston: South End Press, 1983.

Goodman, Robert. *The Last Entrepreneurs: America's Regional Wars for Jobs and Dollars.* Boston: South End Press, 1982.

Institute for Labor Education and Research. *We are Not the Problem!.* New York, 1982.

Lawrence, Anne and Chown, Paul. *Plant Closings and Technological Change: A Guide for Union Negotiators.* Center for Labor Research and Education, Institute of Industrial Relations, University of California, Berkeley, 1983.

Lynd, Staughton. *The Fight Against Shutdowns.* Singlejack Books, 1983.

National Lawyers Guild. *Plant Closings and Runaway Industries: Strategies for Labor.* Washington, DC: National Labor Law Center.

Parzen, Julia; Squire, Katherine; Kieschnick, Michael. *Buyout: A Guide for Workers Facing Plant Closings.* Office of Economic Policy, Planning and Research. State of California, December 1982.

Slaughter, Jane. *Concessions and How to Beat Them.* Labor Education and Research Project. Detroit, Michigan.

Squire, Catherine. *Fighting Back Against Plant Closings.* Economic Development and Law Center Report, Spring 1983.

United Electrical, Radio, and Machine Union. *The Fight to Save Jobs and Stop Plant Closings.* New York.

Workers' Policy Project. *It's Time for Management Concessions.* New York, 1983.

ABOUT THE AUTHORS

Gilda Haas is an urban planner, educator and activist. A founding member of the Los Angeles Coalition Against Plant Closures (LACAPS) she is presently employed as a deputy to Los Angeles City Councilman Michael Woo.

The Plant Closures Project is a labor-religious-community alliance based in Oakland, California. Formed in 1981, the project helps workers and communities fight plant closures, educates the public about economic dislocation, and participates in statewide, national and international efforts to develop and implement democratic and just economic policies.

RESOURCE ORGANIZATIONS

American Committee on Africa
198 Broadway
New York, NY 10038

American Labor
American Labor Education Center
1835 Kilbourne Place, NW
Washington, DC 20010

Boletin Informativo Puente/
Bridge Over the Border
English: c/o LACAPS, P.O. Box 2618
Los Angeles, CA 90051
Spanish: Puente Calle 4A No. 1848
#14, Zona Central Tijuana, Baja CA

California Newsreel
630 Natoma Street
San Francisco, CA 94103
Distributes films about the economy:
The Business of America; What's Good for GM...; The Fight Against Black Monday; Controlling Interest; It's Not Working

Center for Economic Conversion
Plowshare
222C View Street
Mountain View, CA 94041

Citizens Labor Committee on Plant Closures
3600 Wilshire Boulevard, #2200
Los Angeles, CA 90010

Community Economics
1904 Franklin Street, Suite 900
Oakland, CA 94612

Conference on Alternative State and Local Policies
2000 Florida Avenue, NW
Washington, DC 20009

Corporate Campaign
80 Eighth Avenue, 16th Floor
New York, NY

Corporate Data Exchange
198 Broadway, Room 706
New York, NY 10038

Data Center
Plant Shutdown Monitor
464 19th Street
Oakland, CA 94612

Dollars and Sense
38 Union Square
Somerville, MA 02143

Employment Law Center
693 Mission Street, 7th Floor
San Francisco, CA 94105

Full Employment Action Council
Job Impact Newsletter
815 16th Street, NW
Washington, DC 20006

Industrial Cooperative Association
249 Elm Street
Somerville, MA 94105

Institute for Labor Education and Research
853 Broadway, Room 2014
New York, NY 10003

Institute for Policy Studies
Project on Transnational Corporations
1901 Q Street, NW
Washington, DC 20009

Interfaith Action for Economic Justice
Policy Notes
110 Maryland Avenue, NE
Washington, DC 20009

Interfaith Center on Corporate Responsibility
Corporate Examiner
475 Riverside Drive, Room 556
New York, NY 10115

International Labor Reports
300 Oxford Road
Manchester England M139MS
U.S. address: P.O. Box 82391
San Francisco, CA 94188

Interreligious Economic Crisis Organizing Network
I/ECON Newsletter
15 State Street, Room 507
New York, NY 10004

Jobs with Peace National Network
76 Summer Street
Boston, MA 02110

Labor Notes
P.O. Box 20001
Detroit, MI 48220

Labor Research Associates
Economic Notes
80 East 11th Street, Room 634
New York, NY 10003

Labor Today
1831 South Racine, 2nd Floor
Chicago, IL 60608

Midwest Center for Labor Research
Labor Research Review
4012 Elm
East Chicago, IN 46312

Montanans for Corporate Responsibility
P.O. Box 106
Helena, Montana 59624

NARMIC (National Action/Research
on the Military Industrial Complex)
American Friends Service Committee
1501 Cherry Street
Philadelphia, PA 19102

National Labor Law Center
2000 P Street, Suite 612
Washington, DC 20036

New Jersey Committee on Plant Closings
80 N. Fullerton Avenue
Montclair, NJ 07042

Pacific Asia Resource Center
AMPO & *Rodo Joho* (both English)
P.O. Box 5250
Tokyo International, Japan

Pacific Studies Center
Global Electronics
222B View Street
Mountain View, CA 94041

Plant Closures Project
Work Ethics
433 Jefferson
Oakland, CA 94607

Plant Closure Research Group
Department of City and Regional
Planning, Wurster Hall
University of California
Berkeley, CA 94720

Religion and Labor Conference
818 Roder Road, Suite 702
Silver Springs, MD 20910

Southeast Asia Resource Center
Southeast Asia Chronicle
P.O. Box 4000-D
Berkeley, CA 94704

Southerners for Economic Justice
P.O. Box 3840
Durham, NC 27705

The Resource Center
(Latin America and the Caribbean)
Box 4726
Albuquerque, NM 87196

Transafrica
Transafrica Forum
545 8th Street, SE
Washington, DC 20003

Transnationals Information Exchange
(TIE-Europe)
TIE Report
Paulus Potterstraat 20
1071 DA Amsterdam, Netherlands

Tri-State Conference on Steel
130 East Eighth Avenue
Homestead, PA 15120

United Nations Center on Trans-
national Corporations
DC2-1250
United Nations, New York 10017

Washington Office on Africa
110 Maryland Avenue, NE
Washington, DC 20002

Women and Global Corporations
Project/Newsletter
Nationwide Women's Program
American Friends Service Committee
1501 Cherry Street
Philadelphia, PA 19102

Work, Economics and Religion
United University Church
University of Southern California
1817 W. 34th Street
Los Angeles, CA 90007